Walking the Tideline

By Caroline Kurtz

CATALYST PRESS
Texas, USA

Text Copyright © Caroline Kurtz, 2025

All rights reserved.

No part of this book may be used or reproduced
in any manner whatsoever without written consent
from the publisher, except for brief quotations for reviews.
For further information, write info@catalystpress.org

In North America, this book is distributed by
Consortium Book Sales & Distribution, a division of Ingram.
Phone: 612/746-2600
cbsdinfo@ingramcontent.com
www.cbsd.com

In South Africa, Namibia, and Botswana,
this book is distributed by Protea Distribution.
For information, email orders@proteadistribution.co.za.

FIRST EDITION
10 9 8 7 6 5 4 3 2 1

ISBN 9781960803177

Library of Congress Control Number: 2024942057

Wait Without Hope

I said to my soul, be still, and wait without hope
For hope would be hope for the wrong thing; wait without love,
For love would be love of the wrong thing; there is yet faith
But the faith and the love and the hope are all in the waiting.
Wait without thought, for you are not ready for thought:
So the darkness shall be the light, and the stillness the dancing.
Whisper of running streams, and winter lightning.
The wild thyme unseen and the wild strawberry,
The laughter in the garden, echoed ecstasy
Not lost, but requiring, pointing to the agony
Of death and birth.

T. S. Eliot, *East Coker*

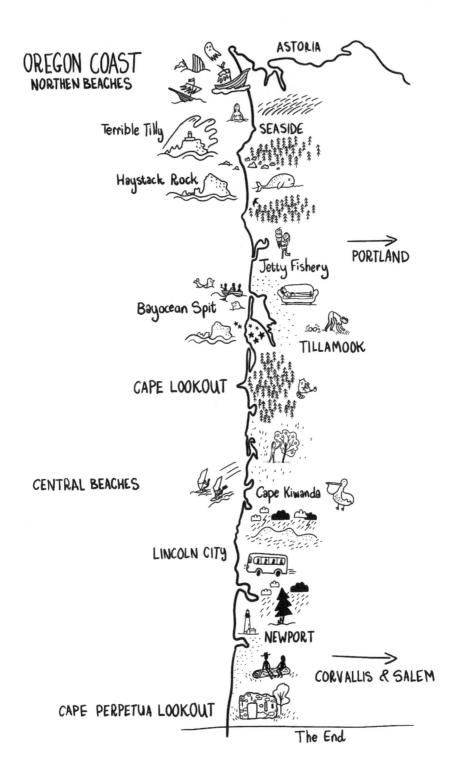

Chapter 1

A year after my husband Mark died, I set out walking south on the Oregon coast. I walked from Astoria, at the mouth of the Columbia River. I carried my tent, my bedding, some food, one book, a change of clothes, and a notebook in a 35-pound backpack. This was to be a pilgrimage of closure.

I had learned about loss in the past year alone: that loss is final but often doesn't feel that way; that I could never go back to my life the way it was but I still wanted to; that the longing for a marriage that had been so far from perfect could feel so very sharp.

The beach morning on my first day out was full of sunshine and water-laden breezes. Sand pipers darted here and there, indifferent to what I carried as I walked. I'd learned about that, too. The hole that had opened up in me and filled with grief was invisible to everyone else. Again and again in the past year, the invisible had collided with the visible. Weather and other people went on around me, unchanged. Even my own body did what it did, unshaken, as emotions convulsed me. Now it was time to bring my inner and outer selves back together and find my way to a life that could feel automatic and pleasing, even without Mark. There on the beach, the tide would come and go, sandpipers would hustle along the tideline. I might see how to live an unselfconscious life, accepting what is.

That first day, I was facing the long stretch of beach between Astoria and the town of Seaside. It was only twenty-three minutes by car, but too far for me to walk. I would have to camp on the beach that night. I hoped one of the day-sites along the way would have water, but I had filled both of my water bottles to the brim just in case.

Wet sand gave under my feet in my brown hiking boots. *Walk at low tide*, the guidebooks say. Walking too high, the drying sand shifted away under my weight. Too close to the waterline, my boots squelched and sank into the waterlogged edge of the tide. I found what the books described—at low tide, a wide band of sand still packed tight and holding the perfect amount of moisture. It gave under my weight, but only slightly. The sand was unbroken except for light tread marks that trailed out behind me, crisscrossed by three-toed bird prints.

The ocean sloshed, as though we were in a shallow bowl, not on the surface of a huge arc, held there by the cosmic magic we've named gravity. It crept closer, covered with foam and lace, then backed away again, an eternal approach and withdrawal.

The sun hung high on my right. Bubbles floated up through the sand and popped where the ocean reached its limit and turned back. Sandpipers snatched up sand fleas that didn't burrow fast enough. The ocean hissed and foamed. Sometimes the lace on a surge of the incoming tide nibbled at my boots and I lumbered further up on the sand.

Sunlight reflected off navy blue pools beyond the breaking waves. Currents formed flowing rivers of turquoise. A chilly gray shadow raced across the water as a cloud moved across the sun. The ocean never stilled. My mind quieted and I walked in wordless companionship.

The Oregon coast belongs to the people of Oregon. In most places, that also means the people are safe from the vehicles of Oregon. But an internet blogger, Bonnie Henderson, had warned that south of Fort Stevens State Park, vehicles are allowed on the beach. Ahead of me, after about an hour of walking, I saw dun-colored shapes I thought were tents. Rafts were being rowed to shore. The scene changed slowly, in gradually shifting perspective, as I approached. Men jumped out, and pulled the rafts up onto the sand, collapsed them, and hoisted them into what I now saw were camouflage vehicles. They drove away.

As I got closer, I could see red crosses on the doors of the one truck remaining. It was deeply sunk in the sand. Soldiers were digging around the tires with collapsible shovels.

"I hope you don't have someone injured in there!" I shouted, over the sound of the surf.

A man straightened and laughed. "It's just an exercise. The only emergency is getting this out of the sand before the tide comes in." The engine roared the and the tires spun, digging deeper. The men with shovels shouted to the driver and went back to work.

I looked back every few minutes, wondering what would happen and who would be blamed if they didn't get the truck out. But of course, they did. I thought back to one of my training walks in Central Oregon, when I had stopped to watch a road crew chain up and lift a huge plate of steel high into the air. It dangled on a hook at the end of the steel boom on a huge machine. The driver lowered it vertically, slowly and carefully, into the trench the men had dug with some other machine. My heart had flooded with gratitude for the physical strength and inventive problem solving that men can bring. It was a strange moment for a feminist like me. And with it had come regret. Mark would have stood with me and watched, fascinated. He, with all his strength, his ability to repair or build anything, was gone.

On the beach, the waves crept in and back relentlessly. My legs tired.

By noon I had walked the eight miles to Sunset Beach Recreational Area. My feet ached. I waded up through deep, dry sand and gratefully shed the pack.

When I was a child growing up in Ethiopia, my dad, two sisters, and I had once walked from the lowland air strip with the traders and their pack mules, about 32 miles up the escarpment. When I tired of walking, I rode. When the muscles of my inner thighs ached, stretched and jostling astride the saddle, I walked again. Unlike our Jeep, which was refilled by a dump of fuel, the mules walked a half day and then slowly refueled by grazing. On this pilgrimage, I was going to be like the mules. My days would be planned around my stamina and the ebb and renewal of my energy.

I stretched my shoulders, and looked around, surrounded by seagrass, sand, and the hiss of the ocean yards and yards away on the blisteringly bright beach. Fantasy gave way to gritty reality—there was no faucet for potable water at this day-site, and the only shade was a small strip on the north side of an outhouse.

I pulled up a trace of gratitude for shade, any shade, and took out my purple gardening pad. My sister had recommended carrying something soft to sit on. Leaning against the outhouse's warm back wall, I ate crackers and cheese, then dozed. Again and again, I jerked awake, threatening to fall over sideways on the cement.

By four, my feet felt normal again and the tide had started out. I shook out my stiff legs. I dug out the map. If I walked for another hour, I would be able to reach Seaside in one day instead of two. I wouldn't have to worry about water for a second night on the beach. I struggled back into my pack and stumbled down to the tideline, to the band of magic sand, my rhythm, and the ocean's company.

Other than shouting to the soldiers, I hadn't spoken all day. I began to sing one of the first folk songs my sisters and I had taught ourselves on the guitar. *The Water is Wide* and the ship knows not if it sinks or swims. The air cooled. I thought of other melancholy folk songs we used to sing together. The waves turned a darker blue as the sun began to back-light them. There were still hours of sunlight, but I was a footsore mule.

I'd always doubted that birds make something we would call a decision when they flutter out of the sky onto a wire. Now, like a bird, my body alit without a decision. I lay back in the warm sand. I wiggled until it nested me. I felt, for the first time, how this pilgrimage would take the shadow-shape of my life. Nobody had told me to keep walking. No one would complain about my cold leftover supper. I was free to please myself. Gratitude washed in.

Only moments later, it washed back out and left me adrift. How was being alone here so different from being alone at home? I rolled onto my stomach, shaped the earth to myself again, and rested my forehead on my hands. My cheek pressed against the sand. When I finally found that mute energy of life-force again and got up, I was covered with sand, gritty and sticky with salt.

I pulled out my sleeping bag and piled it carefully onto my purple pad. I stretched out the tent and then found the loose sand so deep that stakes had nothing solid to bite into. I didn't bother with the rain fly, which would have pulled up at the slightest breeze.

I thought about skinny dipping in the ocean, but gulls were swooping and sand pipers were dashing around me, their naked bodies fully covered in feathers, and I felt inexplicably shy. While my freeze-dried supper soaked, I walked down to the tide line and waded out into the surf. The numbingly cold water drove the last ache from my feet and calves.

The sky pinked as I ate. But the sand was like water; it had seeped into everything. I found if I mashed my food instead of chewing, the grit didn't grind between my teeth. Soft gray shadows set off the rosy sky and ocean. A low row of clouds rose like a cliff across the horizon. The sun dropped toward it, growing bigger as it fell. I rinsed my pan and my clever little spork in the surf.

In my tent and the puffy sleeping bag, I drifted, almost asleep. A moment of terror startled me awake. A half-dreamed sneaker wave was approaching and would sweep me away. Like Mark's cancer, I wouldn't see it coming. I would thrash frantically in the dark, tangled in my sleeping bag and tent. No one would help me. No one would know.

I lay in the dark, settling my racing heart. I reminded myself that I was at the top of the beach, where a dune and the sea grass began. The sand was loose, high above the tide line. It hadn't seen water for a long time. My breathing slowed again.

I woke with the light. When I unzipped the nylon flap, a triangle of sky peaked through, clear and pink, reflecting sunrise on the other side of Oregon. The sea was rosy, this time with twice-reflected light. I stripped and walked naked down the beach. Mist rose up around me. I gasped out loud as I plunged in, out past the low breakers. Never swim alone, the warnings say. I swam, parallel to the beach for safety, to warm up. Back up the beach, I ate my oatmeal with the last bruised banana. My hair, lying against my shoulders, dried salty and stiff.

After I packed up again, I pushed through the soft uneven sand, back to where it was solid, back to the tide's hushed rhythm and my walking. The sky had lost its blush and turned pale blue, fading almost to white in a band above the horizon.

A few months after Mark died, I'd met a man who said that when his dad died, his mother had taken off backpacking around Europe for six months. "She came home a completely different person."

That's what I wanted. I had been this sad, disoriented *me* plenty long enough.

Chapter 2

I was four years old when my parents took my two younger sisters and me from New York to London on a ship, the USS Elizabeth. From there we hopped in prop planes to Athens, Cairo, Asmara, and Addis Ababa, Ethiopia, where my parents began a twenty-three year-long career working for the Presbyterian church.

After language study, my dad volunteered our family for the church-clinic-school enterprise outside of a remote town called Maji, in a southwest corner of the country. Our grass-roofed home sat on the edge of a mountainous Ethiopian escarpment. We looked down from eight thousand feet to the lowlands that merged into Kenyan game plains and the South Sudan's savanna, which is arched by a wide flat sky. My sisters and I ran and played on the lush hillsides. We filled workbooks and learned to read; we sprinkled our sentences with words from the two African languages we heard around us. We learned Bible poetry and sang hymns until we had the vocabulary of people five times our age.

When I was ten, I went alone to a mission boarding school in Addis Ababa, five hundred miles from home. My sisters joined me, one each year. We climbed the aluminum ladder to the C-47s that the US Army in Europe had given the government of Ethiopia to start an airline. The air was hot and dry at the airstrip on the plains. The grass grew shoulder high and we often saw ostrich, gazelle, and zebras. We tearfully waved to our remaining family out the small greasy windows before take-off.

When I was sixteen, I met my husband Mark at that boarding school. His dad was a doctor in an Ethiopian town west of the capital. From the time Mark saw me climb off the bus from the Presbyterian headquarters, he wanted me. I wasn't interested in Mark at first, and in fact, I went with his cute roommate that first year.

I was vivacious and pretty. I was athletic and intellectual and popular. Mark was more the silent, brooding type. My mom quoted Shakespeare's Julius Caesar, "Yond Cassius has a lean and hungry look."

Mark scared me a little. He was the guy who, when we played basketball every afternoon in the tropical sunshine and dust of high-altitude Addis Ababa, would holler when someone missed the pass or fluffed the easy lay-in. I didn't want to play basketball with the boys anymore once we started going together. Mark was shocked at that. "I would never get mad at *you!*"

We were young. We both believed him.

The withdrawn boy I'd seen in class, in the dining hall, and after school opened up once he felt safe with me. He had a lot to say. He was smart. He had a subtle sense of humor. He enchanted my mom after all, when he came for Sunday lunch. He walked into the kitchen, a seventeen-year-old boy, and asked, "What can I do to help?"

After we graduated, we went to different colleges—he in Ohio and I in Illinois. When we both ended up in off-campus programs in Washington DC junior year, we laughed that it must be Presbyterian predestination. We'd both been misfits in late '60s college culture in the States. We'd missed too much, we were oddballs, white kids who'd grown up in Africa, Christians still. We hadn't heard—or believed—that God was dead.

By the time we met in DC again, I'd stopped sleeping with my hair rolled up on curlers and it had grown long and straight. Mark had attended a vigil, carrying a candle and reciting the name of a Latino soldier who had died in Vietnam. It was the dawning of the Age of Aquarius. When Mark came to pick me up at the brownstone where I was living, I was braless. He took me boating among the cherry blossoms on the Potomac.

The Beatles told us all we needed was love.

We got married in the back yard of a professor's house after college graduation. I wore a dress made from Ethiopian fabric; our few guests wore bellbottoms and peasant dresses.

Mark and I quickly learned that it was going to take a lot more than love. Our first used car threw a rod two weeks after we bought it. Our first home, on a farm in SW Minnesota, went up in flames and burned all our mementos of Ethiopia and the expensive record player Mark had built.

I discovered that he would get mad and holler at me.

He discovered that my ebullience was offset by a deep fear that no matter how hard I might try, I'd never be good enough. I could fly high. I could also descend into melancholy and weepy, dramatic insecurity.

In high school, I thought Mark's shy ways had fallen away under the glow of my love. It turned out he was always and forever going to be withdrawn and mostly silent in any kind of a group. He would never make friends easily.

In his last job, as facilities manager of a small private school, the grounds-keeper he supervised told me, "We can always tell when you're traveling. Mark has a daily quota of words. When you're away, he spends them on us. When you're home, he saves them for you."

And yes, Mark hated that I traveled for work. I was his person, and he wanted me around. He was only one of my people, because I needed more scope, more adventure, more attention.

We worked it out over the years. Those pointy edges that bumped and bruised at first got knocked off. I could always bulldoze him with words when we fought. He fought back by going silent and far, far away. But we always found each other again, often in bed. We then slept spooned, turning in tandem, breathing in the smell, the pheromones, the mysterious earthiness of the other's body. Our physical bond grounded us. Or as Mark put it, sex was the WD-40 of our marriage.

At his best, Mark was sweet, vulnerable, and affectionate. He had many virtues. He could fix anything, build anything, put his kids to work, teach them how to drive a nail or a car. He would read to them at night in bed. He would endlessly build Lego castles with them. We were the Kurtz-Rasmussen family, K-Ras for short: Caroline and Mark; Miriam, Jesse and Kenny.

When Mark and I were turning forty, we packed them up and went back to Ethiopia to work for the Presbyterian Church, now alongside the Ethiopians our parents had healed and taught and prayed with. We spent twelve years there in eastern Africa, and our kids turned into richly experienced cultural misfits like we had been.

After seven years in Addis Ababa, we were transferred to Nairobi, Kenya. Our new assignment was to work with South Sudanese who had fled to Kenya to escape the civil war that was tearing their land and peoples to shreds. It was there that I began traveling for work. It was there that Mark learned what he couldn't fix—an African church's financial mess. He descended into rage and depression.

Mark went to the bar one night at a Mombasa resort, and thus fortified, told me that he was leaving me. He moved into our guest suite. In the morning, two days later, he humbly asked me to take him back. "I woke up in the dark and realized how lonely I would be."

I put him on a ninety-day probation, and demanded that we stop having the same fight over and over. We each got a notebook and hammered out who was to blame for what—blame accounting was very important to Mark. We had to agree on the percentages. I was very firm that no one was fully responsible for any of the mistakes and betrayals and disappointments we had subjected each other to. Peace was only going to be found with a mix of humility and math.

We managed to agree, close enough, and renewed our vows on Y2K New Year's Eve. I bought dozens of beeswax candles in case the Nairobi grid collapsed. After our ceremony, we stood outside with our teenaged kids and their friends, counting down, watching the skyline. We all cheered when midnight came and the city lights didn't flicker.

The South Sudanese Presbyterian Church leaders then fired Mark. We came back to Oregon, and he got that perfect last job as facilities manager at the school. When he worked his magic, his

staff would ask what kind of a fix it was—an American fix, meaning he had bought the part, or an African fix, meaning he had made it himself.

But Mark fell into a deeper, longer depression in 2009, one that read again like silent, icy anger. My dad, who had become like a father to Mark, had a brain tumor and was dying. I was preoccupied. Mark thought he was losing us both.

The kids were grown, and this time I was the one who thought about leaving. I went on a retreat and met with a nun trained as a spiritual advisor. I meditated and listened for wisdom beyond my own. I hesitated long enough, and Mark's despair lifted. Loyalty had built up between us, even if sometimes the edifice shook and shuddered. Even grievous violations of trust couldn't break our bond permanently.

But then, Mark was diagnosed with a cancer that had already metastasized. We signed the papers selling our small West Salem farm on the July afternoon of our forty-first wedding anniversary. I did most of the packing up and moving as his pain increased. I ran him to doctor appointments, got his meds from the pharmacies and, too soon, got him on hospice.

One evening in August, I misunderstood his directions on the way to a friend's house and Mark hollered at me. I pulled off the road. I told him I would care for him no matter what, but it was going to be up to him whether we would do this in love or in our worst, tried-and-true scratchy way. That was our last fight.

Mark died in October.

Six months later, my sister Jan told me about the Camino Santiago and gave me her travel guide to read. That was just what I needed, I thought—a pilgrimage—to solemnize the end of my first year of widowhood. A heroic act that would jump-start the future. I wanted to walk from Portugal to Spain. It didn't work out that way. Instead, I walked the Oregon coast from Astoria to Yachats, pronounced so it rhymes with *ha-hots*. I was sixty-four, and I had never backpacked before. I look back now and wonder, *Who was that woman?*

Chapter 3

My kids had taken a dim view of my Via de Santiago pilgrimage idea. And a pastor-friend pointed out that Portugal had nothing to do with my life, shared between Eastern Africa and Oregon. But I kept insisting: Portugal did make sense, smack between the two poles.

Maybe, as I look back now, I wanted something that didn't have to do with any other part of my life—the almost-half-life I'd lived in Africa, the twice-as-many-years I'd lived with Mark than the years I'd lived without him. He'd been a steady anchor for my overly emotional self, a partner in all those years of working in Ethiopia, Kenya, South Sudan and our small Oregon farm. I'd been plunged into retirement by his care and his death. Nothing fit together any more. Everything rattled. Why not Portugal?

It was only when I learned that hot, dry Portugal is wet and cold in the fall that I gave up the fantasy of pilgrimage on the ancient Camino de Santiago. My heart already felt drippy and cold. But I needed some way to embody the end of the first year alone, something to help me turn away from my past and instead look up to see my future.

I remembered wading in the stream below the waterfall where I'd grown up in Maji, Ethiopia. Angular rocks in the streambed dug into the bottoms of my feet. In frigid water, eight thousand feet above sea level, goose bumps ran up my legs. I held up my pant legs and lurched upstream, laughing with my sisters, all of us laughing and shivering with the thrill of the risk.

That's how I wanted to meet my new home, my new singleness, my new friends and companions. I had to believe that the river would bring them down to me if I was willing to struggle upstream to meet them.

I began planning my pilgrimage by reading, as I always do. I read *On Pilgrimage* by Jennifer Lash, who walked the Camino in remission from cancer. I read *Wild*, by Cheryl Strayed, who walked the Pacific Coast Trail. Someone gave me a copy of the movie, *The Way*. And then I discovered something I'd never heard of for all my years in Oregon—the Oregon Coast Trail.

When I tell people I hiked on The Oregon Coast Trail, they say, "Oh! The Pacific Coast Trail!" No. The OCT. A trail that is not famous and not very well organized. It runs along the edge of the Pacific Ocean for 425 miles, from the mouth of the Columbia River to the California border. To be honest, walking the OCT means not only walking along the beaches and up over the headlands, but also on the non-shoulder of Highway 101. Because there are sections where bluffs crowd the shore that closely. Cars and RVs careen by, driving too fast, made impatient by the curves and narrow road because they've gotten used to traveling the freeways.

We Oregonians love our rugged coast, with its equally rugged weather. But Mark and I forgot about the chilly weather after we'd worked for years in eastern Africa, vacationing on Great Rift Valley lakes in Ethiopia and in Mombasa, Kenya. When we came back to Portland for our daughter Miriam's summer wedding, we drove out of sweltering city heat one weekend, wearing our Portland-appropriate shorts and t-shirts, to visit friends on the coast. We'd forgotten that it isn't until a warmer ocean current swings up from California in September, displacing the arctic waters of Canada and Alaska, that weather on the Oregon coast warms up.

Down on the beach that day, teenagers played beach volleyball, wearing sweatshirts in the wind. They flung Frisbees up and down the sand. Mark and the boys made one of their fantastic, sprawling sand castles. Mark worked carefully, doggedly, as always. The boys dug at high speed and dashed here and there collecting feathers, pebbles and shells for decoration. I watched them, smiling, wrapped in a quilt. The tide hissed and crept toward their construction.

When the fall days on the Oregon Coast turn warm and clear, children are back in school. Rental cabins sit empty. Only retired folks and locals walk the sunny beaches.

Now, I googled the Oregon Coast Trail from my tiny rental house in Portland, looking for books on, ads for, podcasts about. Only one helpful thing showed up, a blog written by Bonnie Henderson, who had walked from Astoria to just across the California border. Her travel diary was charming, illustrated with little pen sketches of rocks, weather-beaten trees, and headlands. She included photos; trail conditions; the dangers of walking on Highway 101; information on state campgrounds; and notes on finding the trailheads on the outer edges of coastal towns. I read every word. I printed out a detailed map. I increased the distance of my daily walks.

In Portugal, I would have been in a guided group, our luggage driven from one rustic hotel to the next. On the OCT, I'd have to carry everything. I'd have to camp. But Bonnie would help me. Bonnie and my youngest sister, Jan.

I'd never felt even a trace of interest in joining backpacking trips with her and her family. Now, she offered to lend me her pack and a lightweight down sleeping bag. I borrowed an ancient pup tent. The nylon rain fly was wispy, made before rip-stop was invented. Touching the sides while sleeping in rain would make it leak. But it weighed nothing. And it wasn't going to rain on the coast in September.

I took an overnight camping trip with Jan to try out the tent. I couldn't even sit up inside, so I crawled out in the morning and sat cross-legged on a mat in the opening. The air in the forest by Beaver Creek in Gifford Pinchot Forest, Washington smelled of fir needles and ferns mulching in the moist shade. It carried a tang of woodsmoke from the campfires we'd sung around the evening before.

I looked up at the sky beyond the treetops with a thrill of joy. Branches shifted in a breeze I couldn't feel on the ground. The geometry of sky and dark green needles shaped and reshaped in constant motion.

All my years in Ethiopia, camping was the vacation we could afford. When I was a child in the southwestern part of Ethiopia, we camped on the same game plains that had been developed into parks across invisible borders with Kenya. Dad would drive the Jeep, loaded with everything we'd need, down the escarpment to lowlands, hot, dry, and wild.

We camped by a stream. Dad went for a swim one day and came up for a breath face-to-face with a cape buffalo. On another day, my sisters and I saw a small crocodile at the bottom of a pool near the bank, and dropped pebbles onto its back in a childish attempt at cross-species communication. I wouldn't play in the water upstream that evening. I was sure the croc's mother would be angry because I'd annoyed her baby. She would come for me. She would have her revenge. I had read too many fairy tales.

Five or six years later, I had turned into a teenager working on discovering my unique self—not content to just be oldest sister of five. I stayed at camp to read while the rest of the family went on a hike. The peacefulness delighted me until the quiet went on too long. The world around me turned eerie, as though I were the only sentient being on earth. I put down my book and walked out of the scrubby tree-cover by the river, along the dusty track we'd driven in on. A flicker of movement on my left stopped me. My heartbeat throbbed in my neck. A Grant's gazelle was watching me, almost hidden in the shoulder-high grass, her ringed horns dark spikes above her head.

Only about ten feet apart, we looked at each other, absolutely still, absolutely silent. We looked much longer into each other's eyes than I had ever looked into the eyes of another person. I was not the only sentient being on that plain, in the grass, under the sun.

We looked at each other until I stepped forward slowly—looking wasn't enough, I wanted touch. One step. Two steps. Then she tensed and bounded away. No longer lonely, I went back to the dust and the shade of our campsite.

After my night in the pup tent on Beaver Creek, enchanted by the morning among Douglas firs, I took a trial overnight backpacking trip with Jan's family. I was afraid I'd hate the ache of the pack on my shoulders. It was a big surprise that my backpack would actually be carried by those big, competent muscles in my thighs. As the trail grew steep, Jan showed me that I could loosen the shoulder straps completely. Their job was to hold the pack against my body—to keep it from falling away—and if I was tilting forward to climb, I hardly needed them at all.

The quiet rhythm of walking hypnotized me. I stopped and looked up from the path at my feet. Green meadow stretched on either side, the granite ahead was a silhouette in silver against uninterrupted blue. I lifted into another state of being. The world surrounded and protected me. It promised to go on being what it is, unrattled by my emotions, unshaken, unchanged. In it, I could be what I was.

I wanted more of that moment. If I understood it, if I knew my place in this vast world, I would know how to rebuild my life. In the fall, I would backpack on the OCT.

Back in Portland, I planned out the summer to get ready. I skulked through the aisles of REI, avoiding the eyes of anyone who wore the REI vest. Anyone who might be busy and brisk, who would ask if they could help me. I couldn't make decisions on command.

When I got stuck in one department, I drifted to another. I read the ingredients of dried food packets. I weighed the merits of different tiny stoves. I studied the blow-up mattresses—weight? Size? I wandered for over an hour. I finally circled back and chose four freeze-dried meal packets, a stove, a gas canister, and a charming little cooking pot. I bought a narrow, feather-weight blow-up mattress made of the same stuff as foil emergency blankets. It would rustle in the night when I shifted, but there would be no one else to be disturbed.

I went back another day and bought my brown hiking boots and Darn-Tough socks. At The Next Adventure store, in their used

equipment basement, I found a merino wool sweater with a hood. I looked for shorts, but bought a khaki nylon skirt instead, and a pair of lined nylon warm-up pants with zippers at the ankles. Three t-shirts, a wool cap for evenings, a brimmed hat for sun—I was outfitted.

I read how backpackers manage with so few changes. *Wash clothes with Castile soap 100 feet from streams and rivers. Pull your damp clothes into your sleeping bag. They will dry with your body heat overnight.* I could do that. Or, people go grubby. I could do that, too.

After I bought and borrowed everything I needed, I studied how to pack—more art than science. The soft things go on the bottom (clothes, sleeping bag). Heaviest in the middle, with core muscles to manage them (tent, cooking equipment). Food between the shoulder blades. Sweater at hand on top. Snacks and water at the side in special pockets.

Tucking things in, I thought of Mark. He had had clear communication lines through his hands to the physical world. He packed our car in a Zen state when we traveled, the moving van when we left the farm. I'm not good in that three-dimensional way. It sounded easy, obvious, how to fill the backpack, but I had to start over several times.

And every day that Portland summer, I walked. I had walked and walked throughout the months since Mark died. For someone who had always wanted to talk, it was strange to find myself in a restlessness so visceral. Walking gave me something to do other than thinking. It tired me. Maybe it helped me sleep.

I walked in Bend, a town in Central Oregon with sixty-five miles of trails, where we had moved to live with our son Jesse and his wife when Mark got sick. I stayed for few months after Mark died, then flew to live with our daughter Miriam and her family in Nairobi. There, I walked on back streets, mostly to Java House, where, often as not, I ordered passion juice, just as I had with Mark when we lived there.

Once I moved to Portland, where friends and siblings lived, I walked on the city's one hundred fifty-two miles of urban and urban-forest trails. One began near my rented house, crossed Columbia Boulevard, passed the water treatment plant, and ran to the slough along the northern edge of the city. I walked those miles regularly, training for the Oregon Coast Trail in September.

As I walked further every day, Kelly Point Park became a target destination for my training. Out on the North Portland peninsula, the Willamette River runs along one side of the park and the Columbia River runs along the other. They meet at the tip. Early in our Portland years, Mark and I had discovered Kelly Point Park.

The park was named for Hall Jackson Kelly, one of the most prolific 19th century promoters of the Oregon Territory. Kelly published over forty pamphlets, made presentations to Congress, and was mostly ignored. In his seventies, he published *A History of the Settlement of Oregon and of the Interior of Upper California, and of Persecutions and Afflictions of Forty Years' Continuance endured by the Author.* The park's website says he was a bit deranged.

One of Kelly's visions was to build a city on the tip of the peninsula in spite of frequent flooding. In fact, the very tip of the present peninsula was once an island belonging to the Port of Portland. As the rivers were dredged, silt was dumped until the island connected to the city. In 1984, the end of the peninsula became a park, and Hall Jackson Kelly finally got his notoriety. None of us get to choose how we'll be remembered.

Finally, in mid-August, I felt ready to test my back and feet with a walk equivalent to a day on the OCT. I tucked lunch into the flap at the top of the backpack. I filled my water bottle. I laced up my well broken-in hiking boots and set out for Kelly Point Park.

I saw my neighborhood differently as I walked through, wearing a pack. Portland is a flower city. Some neighbors plant elaborate cottage gardens on every square foot of their yards. Others poke a rhodie in here, an iris in there, and the grass crowds in as their vision for landscaping wanes. Most Portlanders let their grass go during our summers, so dry, so contrary to the year around rain the rest of the country imagines.

Yards that hadn't been mowed recently smelled faintly like hay fields in the warm breeze as I tramped by.

Chapter 4

Mark had been strong from all his physical labor as a contractor, with wiry arm muscles, solid thighs. But he avoided exercise for the sake of exercise. He'd go with me on a stroll now and then, but he complained that I walked too fast. It wasn't romantic. In life, he had never changed me. I had never changed him. And it wasn't because we hadn't tried. Now when I walked, Mark could come with me. And I could walk as fast as I wanted. In truth, I couldn't remember why I hadn't just matched my stride to his.

As I turned onto Columbia Boulevard, I realized that this walk, such a perfect test-run on paper, was not going to be anything like a stroll on the beach. For the next several miles, I would be on a road used mostly for trucking. The asphalt had warmed in the morning sun and radiated heat back up at me. I trudged for an hour along the shoulder with gravel, dandelions, and Queen Anne's lace for company. I tasted diesel exhaust and tar particles in every breath. I pressed on. I would not let Columbia Boulevard ruin my dream.

When I finally reached Kelly Point Park and shade, I shed the pack awkwardly under the leggy trees along the slough. Small boulders that outlined the parking lot had been painted turquoise, purple, and sunshine yellow. The back of my shirt was soaked. I pushed hair off my forehead to let the breeze dry my sweat.

My spirits picked back up as I perched on a bright rock and ate my sandwich. I still had energy at this halfway point. I had clung to my enthusiasm. That seemed an omen, a promise that I could face whatever hardship I would find on the OCT.

Munching a granola bar, I wandered around. Children's art, in a patchwork of small murals, covered a wall. Walking into shade, the air felt cool and fresh, though the slough smelled of mud. When I felt rested, I set out for home, about seven miles away.

I learned a lot that day. I learned that my energy at the halfway point was not data for predicting the second half. I learned that I couldn't walk fourteen miles. I learned how badly my feet could hurt. For the record, Epsom salts don't take away pain. I had learned, but would have to learn again, that we only think we know what we're doing when we set out.

Stumping home from Kelly Point Park, every step a torture, I got so desperate that, if a Portland TriMet bus had gone by, I would have gladly climbed aboard, thrown a five-dollar bill in the till, and not asked for change. For a perfectionist and a tight-wad, that would have been a powerful collapse of my dream. I even thought of calling a taxi, but was too ashamed.

I crawled into bed the minute the sun went down. The next morning, I read Bonnie Henderson's post more closely and was horrified to realize she'd been half my age when she walked the coast. She'd cheerfully put in thirteen to twenty-three miles a day. She'd averaged seventeen. I read her blog again from start to finish, all her glowing descriptions now darkened by the memory of my misery.

Then I took a nap. The following day, my feet didn't hurt any more. That, at least, was hopeful. Despair began to recede, determination to rise.

I orbited alone those days, out on the western edge of Portland, missing the constancy of Mark in every corner of my life, not yet able to connect solidly to anyone else. So, I sat down again with Bonnie, even if I had never seen her face and only knew her from dancing bits on a computer screen. I had begun to think of her as a wise friend and guide, honest and impersonal. Someone who wasn't afraid to deliver bad news. With Bonnie's help, I wasn't going to give up on my pilgrimage yet. It was time to attack the OCT with an excel sheet.

I'd had a lifetime of practice bringing order to chaos. My mom hung a plaque in her kitchen: *Relax, spiders. I keep house casually.*

By the time I turned ten, she had routinely put my inborn sense of order to work sorting the debris left lying around by a family of eight.

Bonnie had walked from one state campground to the next, camping all the way. What if I walked half as far each day and camped on the beaches? It's legal to camp on Oregon beaches, Bonnie said. However, not within town limits. And camping on beaches would run me short of drinking water. *A pint's a pound the world around*—was I willing to add five pounds of water? Also, without facilities, ad hoc beach camping is not recommended nor sanitary.

On a sticky note, I listed the cute coastal Oregon towns. Could I ditch the tent? Walk from town to town like on the Camino? I did the math. Most towns were also twenty miles apart, tucked cozily between those rocky bluffs that rise so steeply and separate Oregon beaches from each other.

I squinted again at Bonnie's annotated map of the OCT. Was there any possibility that, between campgrounds and towns, I could create my own older-hiker's OCT? I was sixty-four years old, for pity's sake. Half of a Bonnie-Henderson day was eight and a half miles. Eight and a half miles was about where my feet had given out on Columbia Boulevard.

Stopping in towns would also give me motel sinks for washing out clothes. I could slip a silk blouse into my pack for town evenings. A bunch of cafe suppers would mean less food to carry. If I yielded boasting rights for walking the entire Oregon coast, I could get from Astoria to just past the halfway point at Honeyman State Park near the town of Florence. The trek of just under 200 miles would take me from September 8th to October 2nd if I walked 7-10 miles a day.

I spent the whole next day on a new excel with four columns: *Date, Destination, Distance* and *Overnight Plan*. When I finished, I had just three blank spots in the overnight-plan column—the first two nights out from the mouth of the Columbia River, and again in Arch Cape, a tiny beach-house town with no motels, grocery stores, or public bathrooms. The Arch Cape town limits stretched all the way to the headlands, so there, I couldn't even camp on the beach.

Friends had a cabin in Arch Cape. But I sat at my desk with my phone in my hand. Those friends and I had drifted apart some years before. I really didn't want to explain myself. Or listen to what they thought of my hike. Maybe I could just pitch my tent in their yard. But what if they were there when I arrived? That would be awkward. What if they weren't there and I couldn't get water for the next day, over the Tillamook headland? It was all too complicated. I lay down on the couch and closed my eyes.

The next day I turned back to my computer and googled couch surfing. To my delight, a man named John offered "a couch" in Arch Cape. He had lots of good reviews. However, as days passed, John did not respond to my email. I still couldn't bring myself to phone friends or talk through my problem with my sisters. I suspected everyone thought I was a bit crazy. I probably was.

But in the confines of my own mind, my spare, simple chart felt deeply satisfying, as though it could balance me, as a walking stick might, and keep me safe. Never mind those three blank spots in the overnighting column. I had learned through many years of practice not to listen to anxious feelings. My pilgrimage chart was close enough. How mean could the police be to a little old lady in a tent on the beach?

On the grand start date of my pilgrimage, sister number four, Cathy, gave me a ride to the Greyhound Bus station, the drop-off for three weeks alone with a backpack. Like a diabetic who can't feel that the stove is hot, I was numb to risk. And I'd let distances build up until none of my siblings felt close enough to question me.

Cathy and I, with three other sisters and a brother, had grown up with a dad who forged ahead into unknowns and a mom who was both anxious and willing to go along. In their Ethiopia career, us kids in tow, they had experienced everything from infected tropical fly bites to revolutions. Dad walked away from several bush plane accidents and outlived a liver fluke.

Cathy had married a Vietnam vet she met in aviation mechanics classes. They spent a year with a development agency in Honduras and two years in Togo maintaining the 'copters for a UN river blindness eradication program. When they came back to the States, Mark helped them turn a school bus into a camper. They lived for years in that bus, driving to Alaska and Montana, repairing logging helicopters.

In Mark's and my overseas years, we'd coped with frequent power and water outages and shortages of everything from eggs to toilet paper. We'd watched guerillas march in to take the capital and ammunition depot explosions that went up in mushroom-shaped clouds. Mark had had both hepatitis and malaria, including 48 hours of hallucinating on an anti-malarial drug. I had taught in bombed out villages, sleeping in grass *tukels* or out under the sky under mosquito nets. I'd pushed airplanes out of deep mud and suffered 36-hour rides in cast-off school buses on potholed roads.

We'd felt despair over fights that rocked our marriage and almost shook it apart. A friend once told me I seem polite, thoughtful, and slightly compliant, but then you find out I'm a wild woman who lives as though I was born to kill poisonous snakes.

Cathy and I had both lived those kinds of lives. But we'd lived them alongside men who tackled problems with energy and ingenuity. Not unlike our dad. They always found ways through—as long as they were facing logistical or mechanical problems. But esophageal cancer had taken Mark, and now, a year later, Bob was dying of advanced bladder cancer. Cathy and I circled each other warily those days, seeing in each other's eyes things we recognized and didn't want to look at.

At the Greyhound bus station, she lifted the pack out of her trunk and onto my back. She reached for a hug, the choreography made awkward by my hulking shape. She patted my shoulder. I turned away, off balance and slightly tremulous.

The bus labored up into the coast range and the Siuslaw National Forest. Trees hovered in green tinged light. The air in the bus chilled. Heaters whooshed on. I watched hypnotically as we passed mile after mile of Douglas fir trees, with their crusty red-brown trunks and high canopy. Rain began. Big drops hit and ran down the windows, blurring ferns and moss, the rich, rich green of that always moist forest.

I thought of Native American youth, maybe hiking up into this same wilderness in search of a dream, a name, a totem animal. I wanted a new dream. A new name. I wanted to describe this feeling to Mark. Tears ran down my face. Mark was truly gone. My eyes ached. When I had felt all I could bear to feel, I fell asleep.

The bus pulled into Astoria. I claimed my pack from the hold and stumbled, hoisting the thirty-five pounds onto my back. A deep breath tasted of fish and sea gulls. I hadn't pictured myself in my walking skirt and hiking boots at this age in a town, dressed and equipped as if I was thirty years younger, but hunger was going to defeat shyness. I walked, looking for a place I would dare go into. And then I saw a sign for the Wet Dog Café.

I stood just inside the door. Banks of windows in front and to my left looked out over the Columbia River rushing to the ocean. The brown waves rolled by, seemingly silent. Around me ranged an assortment of dinged and dented wooden tables and chairs, a dark polished bar, a scratched-up wood floor and paneling. Here, in the café, I was surrounded by the coastal elements—wood and water. I lay my pack on a repurposed church pew along the front wall rather than set it in a chair at my table like a big blue hiking companion.

From up on a stool at the bar, I could keep an eye on the pack and still see the waves heaving out the windows. I ordered fish and chips and, on impulse, black cherry cider. The waitress acted busy, distracted, and completely uninterested in me or my pack. But when I asked how to get to Fort Stevens from there, she sounded doubtful. "Fort Stevens is a long walk." She gave me my change. "Like about ten miles. Let me call a taxi for you."

The overblown pilgrimage meanings I'd imbued on my plan evaporated as I stood outside waiting. A bus. Fish and chips. Now the taxi I'd scorned on Columbia Boulevard. Mark would have laughed. He'd been so much more practical, so much less whimsical.

But now with him gone, my impulses and I were going to have to make our way together without him. I shifted the pack evenly on my shoulders and tightened the hip belt.

Chapter 5

The taxi pulled up, driven by a young woman. She grunted as she lifted the pack off my back and into her trunk. I told her why I was going to Fort Stevens State Park and what I was setting off to do.

"Oh my god!" she said. "My boyfriend died last year."

I stared at her. I knew—intellectually—that I couldn't be the only person on this earth bereft at this moment, recovering. Losses are common as the rain in Portland. Some of them have to be big.

She said he'd been an off-again on-again alcoholic. "Drove me crazy—just *crazy*!" she said. Finally, she kicked him out. Within a year, he took up with a heroin addict and ODed.

"He was the father of my girl," she wailed. Shouldn't she have forgiven him one more time? For her daughter's sake? Maybe she could have helped him. Wouldn't he still be alive today if she had been more patient?

"We can't know that," I said. We think we can. We think we could have sidestepped loss if we'd been smarter. We should have made different decisions, especially the ones that seemed inconsequential but led to other, bigger mistakes. We should have bit back that sharp word, that rant we just couldn't help. We should have made friends with this person, avoided that one. We shouldn't have moved. But in the moment, we did what we saw to do. How hard it is to face our powerlessness. "Now all you can do is forgive yourself," I said.

We drove silently for a moment. Then she told me her dream of hiking the brutally steep trail to Saddle Mountain, south of there, when the wild flowers are in bloom.

"You could do that," I said. "You know, a saddle is a ridge between two mountains. While you hiked, you could think of yourself moving from your old life to a new one."

"Cool," she said. "So where am I dropping you?"

Would she do it, or was she just being polite to my earnestness, my desperation to believe that we can wrestle meaning out of these events that make us feel so frightened, so out of control?

She didn't know where the Fort Stevens campground was, and I had forgotten whatever Bonnie Henderson said. As soon as we saw the information center parking lot, I told her just to pull in. I was not going to drive around, looking for a camping site, in a taxi, for pity's sake.

Mark always circled, looking for the perfect place to pitch our tent: a site with shade, a clean firepit, not rocky, set apart from the madding crowd, and also near the restroom for his wife, who would have to get up in the night. It annoyed and embarrassed me when he did that. It defied the spirit of camping to try hard to be comfortable. But I did appreciate being close to a restroom. Marriage is so complicated.

As I adjusted my pack once again on my back, the taxi driver slipped her plastic bracelet onto my wrist for luck. It looked like something her daughter must have made in kindergarten, with pink, purple, and turquoise beads and a red one shaped like a heart. Cotton candy colors. Too silly. Too lighthearted. It didn't match the serious mood I wanted to be in. Besides, those plastic beads would end up at the bottom of the sea forever. They would kill curious fish.

I had limited self-awareness about my earnestness, but enough to accept her gesture in spite of it. It was my second awkward parting that day.

After she drove away, I slipped the bracelet off my wrist and latched it onto the top zipper of my pack. There, it looked more like what it was—a talisman of love and good luck from a little girl.

At the information center, a brochure informed me I was at the Battery Russell, a mile north of the campground. Battery Russell is a cement bunker, built for big guns trained out over the ocean. In

1942, a Japanese I-25 submarine fired on Battery Russell, the only attack on the mainland of the USA since the war of 1812.

The Japanese shells left craters on the beach, in the swamp inland, and on a nearby baseball diamond. The battery commander didn't let Oregonians fire back. No one knows why, since that's what they were there for. The submarine disappeared again. Thus ended the skirmish between a bank of cement bunkers in Oregon and Japanese invaders.

The episode seemed absurd now, sixty years later. But at the time, the Japanese and the commander took themselves seriously. That's exactly the problem. We don't know what to take seriously, because we can't guess the future. I wanted to have perspective on my life as I lived it, not years later. But could I be that wise?

I wandered along the one-way asphalt roadways, looking for the hiker-biker section set aside for self-powered folks who are coming in exhausted. Bonnie said hiker-biker areas have no parking spots. They have fluid boundaries between camp sites, and a PortaPotty if restrooms are far away. Usually, they're near the entrance. But where was the entrance? I was apparently coming into the campground from the back. As I walked in the high shade of huge trees, I was still too far inland to hear the ocean; I might as well have been in a big city park in Portland.

I grumbled silently as I wandered. The signage was terrible, something that doesn't much matter when you're in a car.

When I finally found the hiker-biker camp, I backed up to a picnic table and gratefully slipped off the pack. I set my camo tent up against some brush. I blew up my new air mattress, it was small enough I could manage it with my own lungs. I lay back for a moment to catch my breath. It was only mid-afternoon.

I'd camped with Mark more times than I'd camped with my childhood family. He loved to set up and find a place for everything, even away from home. As I roused myself and laid out my pajamas—the long-sleeve t-shirt and leggings—I could see his smile.

A moustache that had been turning gray hid part of Mark's

charming smile. As a teen-ager, when we met, he had hated the Cupid's bow on his top lip. As soon as he got to college, he'd grown the mustache. And when he added a neatly trimmed beard, it gave his chin a stronger look. As he lost his mop of almost-black hair, I thought he grew handsomer. Altogether more distinguished.

On one of our recent anniversaries, he told me he'd been thinking I was just about perfect. We'd pulled into the carport in the van. He was still leaning slightly forward in the dim light, turning off the engine. I turned to him in surprise. I was no longer young and beautiful. It was the nicest thing he'd ever said to me.

"What about me?" he asked.

I wasn't nimble enough in love to break the usual pattern, the slightly scratchy effort we so often made to manage the other's comfort and still hold onto our own. I said yes, he was pretty perfect himself. I said I did hope he wouldn't keep gaining weight.

He was stung—of course he was.

I climbed out of the car feeling ambushed by love. Mark's offering hadn't been unconditional, but riven with his own need for reassurance. Maybe that's how love always comes to us. And that quickly, I'd lost my almost-perfect status.

As it turned out, my fears had little to do with my future. Instead of gaining more weight, he'd died a couple of years later weighing less than 100 pounds.

In the tent, I sat up, hunched over on the rustling air mattress. I needed to walk. To get away from my thoughts.

Heading what I hoped might be west, I looked back, uneasy about leaving my earthly belongings zipped up in flimsy nylon. I had pictured the sand, the waves, the headlands with their deep forests. And the camping. But I hadn't realized I'd be chained to a thirty-five-pound pack. It was like having, as my pilgrimage companion, a four-year-old who wouldn't walk.

Fort Stevens State Park was just south of the mouth of the Columbia River, where west-flowing currents, westerly offshore winds, and fog make the navigation complicated. And with no bay, no shallow spreading delta, mighty Columbia River powers directly into mighty Pacific Ocean. All that watery violence creates a constantly shifting sand bar. A disaster can unfold in the space of a few minutes. They call the Columbia bar *Graveyard of the Pacific*. Since 1792, over two thousand ships have gone down.

The US Corps of Engineers added jetties on the north and south sides, and the Coast Guard dredges the channel. Still, it takes experienced river pilots, sometimes heading out by 'copter to take command in bad weather, to bring ships safely past the bar.

Louis and Clark didn't have to deal with the Columbia Bar, but they ended their exploration nearby at Cape Disappointment, named by John Mears, who concluded the mouth of the Columbia was only a bay. The Coast Guard now runs a world-renowned training center for rough water and surf rescue there.

Lewis and Clark's expedition had approached the mouth of the Columbia eagerly, hoping to find a ship anchored there to resupply them. They were out of food, running short of rum, and their clothes were rotting on their backs. So near, they were forced off the river by a fierce winter storm. They pulled into a cove where a creek dumps in and set up camp in high winds, rain, and hail. Later, Clark wrote, "*About 3 o'clock, the wind lulled and the river became calm, I had the canoes loaded in great haste and Set Out, from this dismal nitch where we have been confined for 6 days...*" Their campsite is now the Dismal Niche Rest Area. I wondered if Merriwether Lewis, who'd struggled with depression all his life, felt like he'd found his spiritual home on the tumultuous coast of Oregon.

I wanted to share what I'd learned with Mark. For forty-one years, we had told each other stories—over suppers, on the road, or in our hot tub on the deck of the farm in Salem. Mark told me about his inventive repairs and facilities manager projects. I told him about what I was reading, my writing, or sagas from my trips away from home to raise money or to visit projects in Ethiopia.

Another fact I tucked away: Oregon had built the first Fort Stevens in 1865 to show their loyalty to the Union it had joined just six years before. Oregon vowed, with a fort made of earth, to guard the Columbia River from invasion by Confederate gunboats or the British navy. How useless and grandiose the gesture seemed, 150 years later. Where could I put these feelings, marveling at the absurdity of a story like that, if I had no one to share them with? They rattled like pebbles in a pocket.

The shady state park opened onto a sandy bluff with waist-high sea grass. Finally, the shushing ocean stretched away from me to the end of the earth. A gust, smelling of salt, lifted my bangs off my forehead. South of me, half buried in the sand, loomed one of those Columbia Bar wrecks, the *Peter Iredale*, a British four-master run aground in 1906.

Her captain had ordered the crew to weigh anchor and wait out high seas, wind, and fog, thinking she was fifty miles further out. The wind drove the ship aground. The captain toasted her goodbye, a hulk now listing in the sand: *May God bless you, and may your bones bleach in the sun.* The steel plates and frame of her bow did look like the ribcage of a beast from an ancient era. But it was rusting, not bleaching.

I sat down and unlaced my hiking boots. I labored across the wide beach through sand that was fine and warm but pressed uncomfortably against the tender undersides of my toes. A bright sparkle reflecting off the waves created a rush of joy that filled my empty pocket.

Chapter 6

The campground at Fort Stevens State Park is one of the largest in the U.S. By the time I got back to my tent, I had walked over five miles. A man had biked in and set up camp next to me, riding from Vancouver BC to San Francisco, he said. He was closer to Bonnie Henderson's age than mine, with short blond hair and long lean muscles that made me think of my son Jesse, who ran the 800 in college. This man's bike was so slim, it looked like any stone on the highway would bend the rim. On that delicate thing, he expected to reach San Francisco before I reached Florence, Oregon.

I unpacked my little stove from its just-right nylon bag, studied the instructions, and screwed it onto the gas cylinder. It snatched the flame from my match and hissed happily, bringing a bit of water to a boil in only a few minutes. I glowed at the stove's tiny efficiency, my wisdom at choosing it at REI. I made camomile tea to wash down my fish and chips left-overs. Fog rolled in from the ocean. The light under the tall trees dimmed. I lingered at the heavy weathered table, enjoying the nuances of light. At home, electricity blinded me to how gently day fades.

Later, with the dark tent hovering just above my head, I shifted and rolled over a couple of times, testing the narrow air mattress and my nest of down in my sister's sleeping bag.

The next morning, I greeted the biker, both of us bundled up and shivering a little. He said no, he hadn't had a good night, his air mattress had sprung a slow leak. He was younger than me, and stronger, but things go wrong. Anyone can wake up grumpy any day, anywhere.

I didn't tell him that I'd been up four times in the dark to visit the porta-potty. There would be no more evening tea on my cute little stove. But I'd been glad of what I'd seen in the middle of the night: the fog had dissipated, and a luminous half-disc had smiled down on me. I hadn't thought ahead about how I was going to be outside to see the moon do what it always does. A different shape every night, it glides across the sky, serene and beautiful.

I wiped dew off the picnic table and set up my darling stove. Then I used half of my paper book of matches trying to light it. Finally, I dug out the instructions again. I stopped breathing as I read and then reread a warning I had skimmed over the evening before: *screw the stove tightly onto the gas cylinder. The fittings are soft brass, and gas will escape along loose threads.* I gingerly twisted it. The fittings gave, almost soft as wax.

I'll buy gas in a camping store in Seaside, I reassured myself. I spooned oats into cold water in my bowl. I waited numbly for them to soften. Cold oatmeal. Yech. Well, it would fuel me.

I was bred to hardship, to making do. Mom and Dad had responded to what they considered a call from God, and raised us in Maji with kerosene lanterns, an outhouse, and a tin-roofed house of stucco mud with a cement floor. They'd sent us off to mission boarding school, trusting that God would take care of us five hundred miles from home, I guess. I'd eaten slimy oatmeal every morning for breakfast there. I could do cold oatmeal now and survive again. I was tough.

The biker took down his tent, stuffed everything into his pannier bags and left without a word. I broke camp and, put my things into their assigned places in my pack. I walked over to the trash bin and, not thinking much, dropped in the empty gas canister with a clunk. My pack would be lighter, anyway. I set out on the wide flat beach south of Astoria with my pack snug against my shoulders and hips and a new thrum of worry. How badly, how quickly, how miserably things could turn from a lark into a slog.

That was the real beginning of my pilgrimage. That was the day I walked past the guys doing their surf training and getting their stuck vehicle out of the sand; the day I napped in the strip of shade behind an outhouse and camped on the beach on the way to the town of Seaside.

After I got up and took my dip in the ocean in the pink mist of morning, I had sat and looked at the beach, stretching for miles in every direction, busy with the tide and the restless birds. I contemplated another breakfast of cold oatmeal. I broke out my bag of granola instead. It was meant to be eaten cold.

As I ate, I watched the tide crawl up the beach and scrape back down. I thought about the book *Transitions*, by a man whose name was ironically William Bridges. He said a life transition feels like setting out to sea, leaving the port we know, bound for a destination we don't. He says the *gray zone* between ports can go on longer than we can bear. I had underlined those words.

When Mark got sick, I had taken time off my traveling job of linking Presbyterian churches in the U.S. with the sister denomination in Ethiopia. Then I quit altogether, too raw after he died, to be away from home, speaking publicly, hosted by church members, making conversation with strangers. Apparently, I had suddenly retired. If I came back from this pilgrimage ready to work again, who would hire a sixty-four-year-old? What would I do with myself, alone all day every day? Does anyone fall in love again at this age, or would I live alone for the rest of my life?

I ate slowly. The tide was still on its way out, smoothing my path to tiny Seaside, about eight miles away. I would pass through even smaller Gearhardt on the way, the hometown of famous chef James Beard.

Shaking sand out of everything and packing up took a while. There was nowhere but sand to set clean things on. I had seen the lights of Gearhart and Seaside from my camp the night before, but as I set out again, the lights were off and there was no sign of my destination.

That stretch, from Astoria to Seaside, is the longest, most boring beach on the Oregon coast. It would be great for sunbathing, beach volleyball, and Frisbee throwing, if we'd give it a chance. But it was completely unpopulated. We Oregonians seem to have a taste for beaches that cuddle between headlands and are littered with huge logs. We like our ocean scenes punctuated with monolithic stones. Or maybe we simply prefer restaurants and cafes to picnics and sunbathing. And as I'd found, the day sites on the long northern stretch of beach offer nothing but seagrass and one-door outhouses.

Eventually, the walking itself, the fine packed sand, the quiet tide soothed me. Maybe that's how it would be. Maybe the simplicity of it would come to feel like enough. I would learn how to live with myself.

Just over a year earlier, Mark had complained of pain. His GP thought it was heartburn. The medicine did nothing. Mark wondered about an ulcer, but I told him the patterns of his pain didn't suggest an ulcer. Finally, after about three months, he asked for another opinion and an internal medicine doctor looked down Mark's throat with a scope.

When the doctor found me where I was reading in the waiting room, his face was sober. I held my breath. He scribbled a crude drawing of the esophagus and stomach to show me where Mark's cancer was. Just there, at the joint. He reassured me. *It's early. He'll make it. He's young.* The doctor said they would hit it with everything—surgery, chemo, radiation.

But just to be sure, he was going to put Mark under again and take biopsies of nearby lymph nodes through the esophagus walls. The doctor directed me down to the cancer clinic to get brochures, print-outs, and contact numbers for support groups but I can't remember how I got there—a stairwell, or did I take an elevator? I can't remember the room or the person in the room, though I'm sure she spoke to me kindly. That was the start of a different pilgrimage.

The first lymph biopsies came back positive for cancer, but the doctor was still optimistic. More tests, more appointments, a date for surgery happened fast. I read up about the surgery, which would remove a portion of both Mark's stomach and esophagus. He'd never be robustly healthy again.

A few months before, he had been downsized from his perfect job at the school. The only thing Mark did in the house on the computer after that was play his online solitaire and look for places to apply for work. He was going to stay on unemployment for as long as he could. He was doubtful he'd find another job.

I watched him, after we learned he had cancer. We related to the future so differently—I always wanted to plan ahead. On New Year's Eve, when I wanted to mind-map the coming year, he'd say to me, *There's going to be plenty to do, I don't need to make up work for myself.* Now, I didn't even ask if he wanted to know more about the surgery. He might have quietly done his own research. But it was clear he didn't want to talk about it.

The doctors gave him one more MRI, and then just one more. A few days later, we met for a briefing with the surgeon. Apparently, this surgeon had trained at the side of an operating table, not at bedsides. He barely greeted us. He walked over to a gray-on-gray photo in a light box and pointed to a spot on the x-ray of Mark's femur. It looked like a thumb smudge. The surgeon kept his eyes on the picture. "This just came back," he said. "There won't be any surgery."

We were too surprised to ask questions. On the way home, Mark admitted how much he had been dreading the surgery. We laughed with relief. But rounding the last gentle hill to the farm, I sobered up. "I wonder if we've mistaken the silver lining for the cloud," I said.

I privately asked our daughter Miriam, a nurse practitioner.

She studied me. "Do you want to know?"

I nodded. I knew already.

"He's saying *inoperable.*"

Miriam and I sat across from each other and wept.

I learned that between five and forty-seven percent of people diagnosed with esophageal cancer survive for more than five years. It depends on whether the cells have already spread beyond the tumor. I learned that esophageal cancer is aggressive and a sneaker

—eighty percent of cases metastasize before they're discovered. I knew that the death rate in the first year looks like a cliff—like the dizzying, stomach-turning view of earth dropping thousands of feet from a spot we'd called Down on Both Sides, the earthen bridge between mountains on the road to Maji, Ethiopia.

Mark's cancer was terminal. I couldn't manage our little farm alone. I set my plan-making self in motion and we spent the next six weeks unraveling our lives. Mark went to a prayer healing event and felt hopeful. The woman talked as though if we prayed right and recruited an army of "prayer warriors" to pray right, God would be forced to send a miracle.

Miriam said, "Mom, it's called a miracle because it hardly ever happens."

I knew that. I didn't have much hope. But I didn't say anything to Mark. I wanted him to hope for as long as he could, any way he could.

Friends sent Mark complicated lists of food to eat and not to eat, visualization exercises, Bible verses to read daily. An Ethiopian friend brought holy water, made Mark stand half-naked and shivering on our porch, and doused him with it. There are many ways to experience loss. But when we can see it coming, we'll dance to any ritual we think might ward it off.

I got rid of the things we didn't need but had collected in our sojourn in Salem. I packed away the basics, including Mark's special popcorn popper and his Italian espresso pot, in case we could start over some day.

On our 41st wedding anniversary, Mark and I sat at our dining room table with a realtor. He passed page after page to Mark and from Mark to me. *Sign here. Initial here. Initial there.* For twelve years, the longest either of us had ever lived in one place, that small Willamette Valley farm had been home for us and thirty chickens, a mama cow and her grass-fed offspring, apple and pear trees, vegetables, and a riparian reclamation project. The names of the native shrubs and trees I planted had rolled around in my mind like poetry:

big-leaf maple, Western red cedar and Oregon white oak; ocean spray, goat's beard, Douglas spirea, rosa rugosa. I had rooted shoots of native willow into the streambed to compete with reed canary grass, which wants to take over the world.

Now I signed my name on real estate contracts and abandoned our animals, the shrubs and trees and vegetables. I hoped a good family would love them. There was no time for me to grieve the farm. Mark's pain was getting worse. It was up to me to get us moved to Bend, a town in Central Oregon, where Jesse and Beth had offered us shelter for the coming months.

The doctor in Salem put Mark on those magical and dangerous painkillers, but he continued to feel pain. He worried about getting addicted. The nurse told him not to worry, somehow pain soaks up and neutralizes the painkillers. It's only when there's no pain to counteract that they become addicting.

Later, the hospice nurse in Bend told him the same thing as they hooked up his morphine pump. I sat in the big reclining rocker I'd bought for him when I thought he'd be with us longer, and watched him doze in a morphine haze. I wondered how it could be possible, what the nurses said about the painkillers. By then, I knew he wouldn't have to worry about addiction.

I also didn't need to have fussed at him about healthy eating.

"People who don't eat dessert aren't living longer," he always said. "They just think they are."

I was glad he'd enjoyed his desserts in the wholehearted way he had.

Mark died in Bend less than three months after we got there.

Chapter 7

Jesse and Beth invited me to stay in Bend as long as I needed to. I was tempted to find a little house and move there. Why not? Without Mark or the farm, I felt untethered, like a helium balloon some child had lost. When I couldn't sleep, I curled up in the big rocker, flipped open my laptop, and made a starred list of furniture on Craigslist—a wrought-iron baking center, an ornate brass bed, old-fashioned couches that looked as though they might actually be stuffed with horsehair. I wanted old things, as though by surrounding myself with them I could also go back to comforting times.

After three months, I flew from Bend's frigid and frost-tipped high desert to the clear skies and sunshine of Nairobi, Kenya, where Miriam and her family had moved. The sunny skies there didn't cheer me. I brooded. Miriam finally declared I was depressed and found me a counselor.

When Mark and I were packing up, we'd talked quietly, dreaming—wouldn't it be sweet if he licked the cancer and we moved back to Portland to the home where we'd lived when the kids were little? We couldn't talk about what I'd do if it was me starting over alone. Mark only said one thing about that. "You'll probably remarry. But I sort of hope you don't. I still want to be special to you in heaven."

I'd laughed and hugged him. "Don't worry. I don't think it works that way."

When the time came, I couldn't face living in the house where we'd raised the kids. Mark had remodeled it in the '80s. His presence, his actual fingerprints, were everywhere. Instead, I rented the tiny place near Cathy, a house that might hold memories for someone else, not me. And that's where my new life really began.

I had lots of siblings. I had always lived with sisters, roommates, or Mark. Living alone felt at first like playing house. I threw myself into it, as though this was an assignment and by being a good student, I could ace it. I didn't ask for help. I didn't need help.

I put foam pads under the feet of the loveseat, where Mark and I had snuggled to watch movies. I leaned all my weight against it, first pushing it against the wall, then scooting it across from the fireplace. I dug a hammer out of Mark's tool box and hung art. I watched a YouTube video and replaced the missing rib in the clothes dryer, just to prove to myself that I could manage. I didn't need a man to take care of my home for me. I was going to take care of myself, like I had when Dad put me on the Ethiopian Airlines C-47 alone to fly to boarding school.

But I'd lost all interest in cooking. That part of playing house had been fun when I was a girl with my sisters, collecting lupin seed beans and grass seed rice for our Teddy bears, pulling the centers from calla lilies for corn on the cob.

Later, I'd cooked for Mark and my children, but only as a chore. Cooking ranked above vacuuming but below folding laundry. On my better days, it might have sometimes risen to an act of service. I was better at grand gestures, not great at the little, friendly, warm ways of holding life together for other people.

Now that Mark was gone, I couldn't summon up motivation to cook for one. Books admonished a tender and nurturing attitude to the child within but I just ate a lot of peanut butter. I baked a potato or a yam. But I did start to eat the dark chocolate I'd bought as people urged me to take care of myself when Mark was sick in Bend. It had tasted then like mud. In my new home in Portland, I nibbled it slowly and savored the bitterness on my tongue.

On the shallow beach north of Seaside and south of Fort Stevens State Park, I trudged along. Just as I reached some peace, the ocean whispering to me as it crept respectfully closer, not threatening the brown walking boots, I saw buildings. I dug out my Oregon Coast

Trail instructions from Bonnie Henderson: *Turn off at a five-story condominium.*

Condominium as landmark on a spiritual pilgrimage. Over and over, I was being invited back down to the ordinary. I didn't want ordinary. I wanted a mystical magical healing. I wanted a dramatic revelation, the golden road to happiness opening before me as it did in the fairy tales.

But what I had was the ordinary. I turned off at the condominium and zig-zagged this way and that through Gearhart, following the map to the Seaside International Hostel, run by a Vietnamese woman named Trung. My feet were starting to ache.

As I'd learned when I walked with the tall South Sudanese on their wide-open plains, it's impossible to limp when both feet hurt. I groused my way past charming cottages with window boxes and cute welcome signs. Too charming. Too cute. All it had taken was one night out with my tiny tent, sunset and sunrise, to turn me into a grumpy ascetic.

I stumbled into the hostel lobby and collapsed on an old couch. When I'd recovered enough to get on my feet again, I stepped up to the reservation desk and coffee bar. Trung, with her black hair cut short, was small, quick, and efficient behind the bar. I filled out the registration form and chatted with her. "I'm walking the OCT," I said. "I'm doing it as a pilgrimage. And everything has turned metaphorical."

"Everything is *always* metaphorical. We just don't notice."

I stared at Trung. Maybe I was on a spiritual pilgrimage after all. Maybe condominiums, charm, and cuteness were only a thin veneer hiding depths I would stumble into if I just had eyes to see and ears to hear.

I padded barefoot back to the lobby after I dropped my pack in the women's dorm room. Following Bonnie Henderson's advice, I asked Trung for a Vietnamese coffee. She told me the secret ingredient: sweetened condensed milk.

In boarding school in Ethiopia, we'd cooked sweetened condensed milk in its own unopened can in pans of water on our hotplates. It turned into a rich brown caramel. I drank the Vietnamese coffee in tiny sips. Each sip flooded my taste buds with delight.

I'd pushed myself, and compressed the first three days of my walk into two days of about eleven miles each. Lying with my feet elevated on a pillow in the dorm room in Seaside, I decided to nurture my inner child with an extra day at the hostel.

However, now that I was in Seaside, I needed to think about cooking fuel again. I shuddered. I had resolutely not thought about how I'd not taken care, not read the small stove's instructions carefully. Once, when I'd written something critical of our boss and accidentally copied him in the email, one of my colleagues said to me, *Does it ever scare you what you're capable of doing?* What else was I capable of doing, out on the trail alone?

I busied myself at the hostel, carrying clothes out to the balcony and shaking the sand out. I washed my t-shirt and underwear in the sink. Finally, I got myself out the door to case the town of Seaside for another canister. Someone else might have rested and nurtured that inner child first, but not this oldest daughter. I couldn't rest until I took care of what was making me anxious.

In Seaside, I found t-shirts, sweatshirts, and kites. Seaside had beach-cabin bedside tables, ceramic seagulls, and the cute welcome signs. Seaside had no camping supplies.

Friends later said maybe a mall somewhere would have had camping supplies. I could have gotten there in a taxi. The truth is, I'm so determinedly self-reliant I didn't even think to ask Trung. In Safeway, I bought protein bars and more cheese.

After the luxury of hot oatmeal in the hostel's industrial kitchen the next morning, I decided my rest day warranted another Vietnamese coffee. For me, it was an indulgence, and indulgences required careful consideration.

Trung fired up the espresso machine. The smell of coffee, rich and musky, reached my nose. I turned on my phone to text Kenny, my youngest, who'd made me promise to check in as I walked. Up came an answer from the stranger I'd written to in Arch Cape, the third blank spot on my list, the final place I didn't have an overnight plan for. I gasped. I told Trung—a man named John, a couch.

"John Markham?" she asked. "I'm on a coastal community committee with him. I know he takes in couch surfers. Let me call him for you."

She greeted him and handed me her phone.

"Do you like pork chops?" John said.

I laughed. Was this a fairy tale riddle?

"All I ask my guests is that they cook for us," he said. "I'll get pork chops. Anything else you'd like?"

I suggested apple sauce.

"I've got apples," he said.

"He's a good man," Trung assured me.

I spent my extra Seaside-day in a glow. Maybe I couldn't count on myself not to make mistakes. No matter, I would be cared for, guided, buffered by the mystery of synchronicities. How amazing it was, really, that the message should come in when Trung was standing there. That I told her, that she knew John, that she had his number and put us in touch.

In the afternoon, I luxuriated in a lounge chair in the backyard of the hostel, on the banks of Neawanna Creek. I'd browsed the take-one-leave-one library in the lounge and homed in on a book called *Happiness* by Richard Layard. I skimmed it in the warm sunshine: how we think *things* will make us happy—the new dress, the new car, the new house. How we quickly adapt and those things become status quo. We move on restlessly, searching for the next jolt of temporary joy.

I copied wisdoms into my soft little notebook. Layard said that there are some things people never adapt to. He mentioned widowhood in his list of miseries, along with loud and unpredictable noise, and caring for a person with Alzheimer's. And another list of good things that never cloy included pleasing sex, friends, a compatible marriage. He said the secret to happiness is to search for those good things, things that you'll never stop enjoying.

I let my mind drift like the creek that flowed by, so close to its destination. Mirror-flashes from the sun on shifting ripples blurred into a mass of sparkles.

That night, I woke at 3:30. I couldn't get back to sleep. I tried not to disturb the roommate, who had moved into the hostel dorm that day, by thrashing around in my bed. Out the window, I saw the bright three-quarter moon. The air in the room felt stuffy.

The book on happiness had said without reservation that the one common strand in what can give us lasting happiness is love. That afternoon on the banks of the creek, when I'd asked myself where I was going to find love again, I'd sensed the only sensible, one-word answer: Wait.

Waiting seemed hopeful and encouraging. It implied finding. Could I wait, as a spiritual practice? I didn't really want to wait. I wanted immediate relief from widowhood, which did feel like a misery.

I snuggled the blanket under my chin and closed my eyes again. I thought about Mark, and began reviewing the whole story of our forty-one-year marriage. The good parts, the hard times. His good side. Mine. His anger. My discontentment and judgements. My inability to stand my ground. Awake like this, I thought of other nights when I couldn't sleep because he lay unyielding in the bed beside me, refusing any touch. Now, I would have gladly waited on my side of the bed. Now I would have been patient, if I could only have had him back. Because always, in the end, Mark thawed and we drew close again.

I finally got up, crept past my dormmate, and flipped a light on in the quiet library.

The sky was lightening when I crawled back into bed. I rubbed my feet back and forth on the sheets to warm them. I fell asleep.

The other woman's alarm jolted me awake. She didn't stir. The alarm cycled on and off three times before she got up and stumbled into the adjoining bathroom. She left the alarm cycling, beeping wildly.

Her lack of thoughtfulness, my disgust—if being around people was going to make me feel more loneliness, the trail beckoned. Instead of eating my lunch at the hostel as planned, I left before the noon low tide. I was going to climb that day, eight miles up Tillamook Head to a hiker camp, a circle of three-sided cabins at the top. I would sleep there on my way to Cannon Beach, a town popular with Oregonians and tourists from near and far, with its wide beach and Haystack Rock. They come to see that giant stone standing in the tide, the tufted puffins who nest on its steep sides, the gorgeous silhouette it makes against the sunset. In 2013, Canon Beach was listed by National Geographics as one of the world's most beautiful places.

At the base of my first steep climb, a charming wooden bridge spanned another creek running to the ocean. I reached it just as a wiry, craggy-faced man in faded jeans appeared at the other side. It was hard to tell his age, his hair hidden under a baseball cap.
He gestured for me to cross. The bridge echoed hollow under my boots.
"I'm Jason Eugene Johnson," he said.
I told him my name.
"You just livin' free?"
"No, I'm on a pilgrimage."
"Caroline, you're beautiful. You smoke the Mary Jane?"
"Not anymore."
"I do. Medical marijuana. I've got multiple organ failure; my pelvis is going and my hips are gone. But I'm still here. I guess."
"You must have a strong heart." I held out my hand to say goodbye. Now I could see the graying ponytail below his baseball cap.
Jason Eugene Johnson bowed over my hand, lingering, and kissed it.

Chapter 8

After Mark's death, when I told my sisters I wanted to marry again, Cathy had shuddered.

"Maybe a boyfriend with his own house," she said. "Marriage? Never!"

But I liked someone warm and musky with me in bed in the morning. I liked laughing, venting, or companionable silence over supper. I liked having someone who welcomed my touch, who hugged me back. It was down there in the book on happiness—love is the magic strand that brings us happiness.

Moving into my tiny rental house in North Portland, I knew that at least I needed more friends. I was settling back in Portland because I had siblings there. I had my writing group. But misery was still only too ready at hand. I missed family chaos, routines, chores. I needed friends to do things with, not just to drink coffee with and commiserate. I needed to keep moving, herding my mind away from all that was new and different and disappointing about living alone. I looked online for meet-up hikes. But I never signed up. What if a stranger asked me why I'd moved to Portland? I would just start crying. Words, how I'd always connected with people, were betraying me, both the silent ones in my head and spoken ones. I needed to be around people, but I couldn't talk.

Maybe dance would work. *Stop thinking. Feel the lead,* my swing dance teacher said. I might not always feel a lead, but I didn't have to be a good dancer to feel the music. It lit my brain, made it feel red and yellow and blue, like the photos of brain studies. No matter how I felt as I walked into the dance hall, I felt new and clear when I walked out. And I wondered. Of course, I wondered, *Would I meet someone there?*

I met several Jason Eugene Johnsons who found me attractive. One man, on a Salsa night, asked if I had come alone. When I said yes, wondering if I should admit it, he asked if I'd driven. Then he asked if I would like to go out for dinner after the dance and drive him home. I was lonely, but not that lonely.

Another man began regularly asking me to dance at West Coast Swing Wednesday dances. He seemed about my age. Maybe a little younger, which was in his favor. Tall, good looking, he usually wore a bandana across his forehead, tied over his gorgeous white hair, to keep the sweat out of his eyes.

Pretty much every man sweated through the back of his shirt in an evening of social dancing—often the front as well. I wasn't a squeamish person, but it took me a while to get used to it. Some men politely changed shirts halfway through the evening. On summer nights, I felt drops of sweat trickle down either side of my own backbone. My arm, when I looked, glistened. When I brushed arms with my partner—well, the only test was whether we had both used enough deodorant. It was pass-fail.

The guy with the white hair and bandana passed. One night he was definitely romancing me, looking into my eyes and smiling slightly. The song was slow for West Coast Swing: maybe he and I *would* find love right-where-we-were, as the song said, there on the Norse Hall dance floor. He was definitely going to ask for my phone number when the music stopped.

We began to chat—I was just getting good enough, those days, to chat and dance at the same time. *Left side turn:* I told him I was the oldest of seven.

Spin and back to center. "Oh! My wife is the oldest of seven, too!"

My hot cheeks turned cold. He had clearly said *is*. After a shocked glance up, I didn't meet his eyes again. I didn't say another word. When the music ended, I nodded my thanks and walked away.

My new women friends peered through the crowd to where I was pointing.

"White hair?" one of them said. "Oh, that's Duke. He's polyamorous. Yeah. Don't do Duke!"

I came home and googled *polyamorous*. We didn't call it that in the 1970s, when I was last single. I'd married Mark, thrilled to be done with polyamorous men.

The next Wednesday evening, I thought I should ask Duke to dance, to show him I had no judgmental feelings. And then I stopped myself. Why would I do that? Duke used his good looks to get dance partners. He led weird moves with unearned confidence. He was very hard to follow.

I was going to have to get tough if I was going to be out there dancing. Stop taking care of men's feelings. I had communicated my own feelings effectively to Duke. He never asked me to dance again.

Another dancer, when I admitted I'd been raised overseas, said,

"We're perfect for each other. You've lived overseas and I'm an immigrant."

I was doubtful that would give us enough in common, but willing to give him a chance. On dates one and two, he filled me in on the wife who'd been unfaithful and left him but demanded alimony for the rest of his working days. He told me the story of another woman he'd taken to an expensive restaurant only to be told that she had no income at all, but a boyfriend for every night of the week to take her out to supper. She assured him she didn't sleep with any of them. It's a weird world out in older-people-dating-land.

For my third date with this man, he offered to cook salmon for me at his house. He set me up on a leather couch so big my feet didn't touch the ground. Waltz was his favorite ballroom dance. He started a waltz video for me to watch.

Wow. A man who loved to waltz and would cook for me. My doubts faded a bit.

Mark had hated when I said we should rotate the cooking. We were both working. Why shouldn't we share housework? Well, where was I when something broke? Didn't he get credit for the man-jobs he did? I backed down and cooked for the next 38 years, as long as Mark cleaned up after supper. It was a workable trade in the kitchen, and he willingly did so much outside the kitchen.

I later understood the only way his mother had shown him love had been with food: a meat, a starch, a salad, and a dessert. The table was set with shining silverware on each side of the plate, the napkin and glass placed neatly on the left with the fork. Supper served on time.

As for dancing, Mark's relationship to rhythm had resembled windshield wipers that start together, get more and more out of sync, and suddenly find their rhythm again on the opposite foot.

Now, given my peanut butter and baked potato diet, this date's attractiveness rose as he called me away from the video with women in ballgowns spinning around the glowing floor. He was carrying a platter of salmon, garnished with lemon slices, to the table.

After supper, he wanted to cuddle. So far, whenever he took my hand, I had only managed for a few seconds before I withdrew it. I only wanted to touch men dancing, when it was prescribed and impersonal. But this was our third date. He seemed nice enough. And he had cooked for me. I nervously rested my head on his shoulder. And burst into tears.

My head on Mark's shoulder had been a comfort. I knew his arms. This man's shoulders, his arms, his chin so near only made me nervous.

The next week, my daughter-in-law Beth miscarried. Jesse wept when he told me. "I don't have a father to help me through this," he said.. And I didn't have anyone who loved my son as I did.

My date called me the next day on a break from work. "Why are you sad today?" he asked.

"I'm lonely. And...the baby..."

"Don't be sad," he said cheerfully. "They're young. They'll have another. And you don't need to be lonely—I'm here!"

I didn't answer. I wanted a man with some empathy. But more, I wanted the depth, the history, the thousands—no, millions—of connections that accrete in a long marriage and stitch together into a complex quilt of dark and light, a weighted blanket that would ground me in my bed at night.

The dance community was full of single men, but men who had been through the wars of marriage, divorce, and spousal support. Their histories and mine did not match. And what I was missing wouldn't come again quickly.

After I said good-bye to Jason Eugene Johnson at the bridge at the bottom of Tillamook Head, I found the trailhead and another park sign: Lewis and Clark had also walked from Seaside to Cannon Beach. Clark kept a detailed journal, noting the flora and fauna they found (with the common-sense spelling that came before Webster). Clark wrote that *some species of pine or fir on the top of the point rise to the emence height of 210 feet and from 8-10 feet in diameter.* He estimated most of the trees were only 100 years old, but saw some that had earlier survived a major natural disturbance.

He called the view from the top of Tillamook Head *the grandest and most pleasing prospects which my eyes ever surveyed, in front of a boundless Ocean.*

At the base of the climb, a sign told me I was about to enter the Elmer Feldenheimer State Natural Area, donated by Marie Louise in memory of her brother. She hoped the forest would enjoy one thousand years of rest, and the trees would live long enough to cover the headland with old-growth timber again. A few of the older ones Lewis and Clark saw are still healthy, now three hundred years old, the sign said.

The trail started right up 3300-foot-high Tillamook Head. I was immediately working too hard to appreciate Marie Louise's precious forest as it rose around me. My glutes had trained in flat North Portland and now threatened to cramp. I hoisted my pack over a downed tree across the path, dropped it on the other side, and clambered over immodestly in my hiking skirt. The rough bark scraped my thighs.

At the next downed tree, I stopped, sat on a stone beside its root

51

ball, stood twice as tall as me, and ate a fig bar. Then I tried crawling under. My pack snagged and caught above me. Sharp bits of forest mulch dug into my knees. The scent of it, still piney, barely pierced through my struggle.

I climbed onward, sweating, my face hot, my breath squeezing past my pounding heart. There was no more meditating on love.

And then I rounded a switchback—voila!—a walking stick just my size, hanging on a twig right before my eyes. I wiped sweat away from them and stared.

Though I hadn't seen another human all day, worrying about how to get help was never on my conscious mind. I gave thanks for an angel in hiking boots who'd left the walking stick for me to come across, not even knowing who I was.

I was especially grateful for the walking stick when I got to the top. The high canopy blocked the sunlight above the trail,, and even in that unusually dry summer there was mud. Some wooden walkways, slimy wet, kept me out of mud holes. But most puddles had to be forded. Hikers had walked around or waded through, making them wide and deep. I mucked along, smelling rot and mold, leaning on the stick to keep from slipping. I imagined myself face down in the mud.

The deeply forested ridge was flat across the top, not peaked, as I'd expected. As the path went on gently undulating, I caught my breath. My legs stopped shaking. Here and there, between tree trunks bigger around than I was, I saw glimpses of the ocean over the edge of the cliff. From these thousands of feet up, the ocean was silent. It looked lacy and pacific, in gentle motion. Floating out in the haze stood the Tillamook Lighthouse. *Yes, Mr. Clark*, I thought. *"Emence"* beauty.

Between mud holes, my head filled with the scent of ferns and mulch, deep old mulch, the bodies of huge trees rejoining the earth they'd grown from. The ground was littered with huge crumbling stumps, deer fern, sword fern, and salal. Awe settled into my heart. I stopped and tipped back my head.

Any lingering thoughts of love, of need, of loneliness dissipated. For a moment, I breathed softly with the giants.

Chapter 9

I came to the southern edge of the ridge and the trail began to descend. As hard as they'd worked going up, my legs now had to brace me going down. They shook. I was afraid I'd fall. Just when I worried that I'd missed a turnoff, I saw the cabins of the Ecola Hiker Camp on a flat spot two switchbacks below me. I got to the camp, shed my pack, and collapsed at the picnic table.

How naïve I'd been. If I'd wanted insights and healing thoughts, I should have gone for three weeks to a retreat center. Labeling it a pilgrimage didn't erase the ache in my feet, the shaking in my knees and thighs, the heavy breathing and heart knocking of a human on a steep mountain.

Without fuel, I was going to be softening my freeze-dried meals in cold water. Yech. Good thing I was prone to asceticism in the best of times. I pulled out my little pan and started some couscous softening. In the forest behind the cabins, late afternoon sunlight pierced through in places. It struck patches of bark, a branch here, a clump of ferns there. It brightened the air in rays, and lit up clusters of flying bugs. I watched them, testing whether the beauty around me was adequate reward for the effort I'd made. Whether beauty, unshared, could satisfy. My breathing slowed. My mind calmed.

I wandered over to explore the cabins, open across the front, with wooden bunks built into each side wall. I laid out my bedding and then walked out to the edge of the bluff. From a boulder I watched the sunset show. The lighthouse below stood in lonely elegance in water that stretched out endless in every direction but mine. The sun turned the entire horizon and the ocean between us peach and fuchsia.

As the light faded, and with it the colors, the lighthouse disappeared into mist. A chilly breeze blew in the faint warning tone of a buoy. I sat there until I was shivering and there was nothing left of the sun but a golden orange glow, like a forest fire at the far edge of the ocean.

A brief squall of sorrow overtook me as I walked back to camp. It was wordless, the grief of loss, the utter helplessness to do anything about it. Stepping forward, because there was nothing else to do as life still stirred in me.

How long would this go on? I had accepted the first year's grief, the missing Mark, the starting of a new life. For a year, grief seemed acceptable, even to people who were silently growing impatient with me, who didn't want to hear about it anymore, who wanted me happier already. I'd started to cocoon my feelings months ago for them. But my future still looked like a huge void. I was still lonely. What did I have to look forward to, in the years to come? And how long would sorrow keep washing in?

I'd hoped for a new relationship, thinking that would stabilize me. Most men remarry within three months of losing their wives. They must be driven by loneliness as well as the logistical difficulty of tasks they'd never had to do before—grocery shopping, cooking, cleaning. My generation of men, anyway, have trouble staying connected to each other.

Statistically, women wait for over a year to remarry. Maybe we feel our grief more sharply. And maybe we also feel some relief from those very tasks. Tasks that seem invisible and go unappreciated. Studies say married men are happier than unmarried. But married women feel more ambivalent. I'd felt ambivalent often during my forty-one years of marriage, but now that marriage had been stripped away, I missed it terribly.

Eating my cold couscous on the heights of Tillamook Head and managing the simple tasks of settling in for the night dislodged my gloomy thoughts. I hung the food bag up on a hook and put the bear spray with my headlamp under a bundle of clothes in my pillowcase.

Use the food bag hook to confound the rodents, Bonnie Henderson said. *They know people carry goodies.*

And before I could fall asleep, something rustled in my pack on the other bunk. I remembered the fig bar I'd left in a side pocket. Help yourself, I thought, and covered my ears. I snuggled deeper into my down nest and planned the next morning. Before I decamped, I would visit the rocky lookout again to see the Tillamook lighthouse in misty dawn light.

Native Americans believed sea spirits lived in under-sea tunnels that open on Tillamook Rock. The sea stack of basalt had looked like a dragon head before the lighthouse was built.

The process of building was fraught. In trying to land and survey, an experienced lighthouse mason from Portland had been swept away. His body was never found. Local construction crews began to whisper that the project was cursed. The Army Corps of Engineers hired a crew from out of state and sequestered them at Cape Disappointment so they wouldn't hear the rumors.

Construction took over a year and a half. Midway, another storm's pounding waves flung rocks and swept away tools and provisions, leaving the crew stranded for two weeks until they could be resupplied. Before construction was even finished, people started calling the lighthouse Terrible Tilly. A week before she went into operation in 1881, a ship foundered on the rock in fog, its only survivor the dog.

None of this was Tilly's fault. She wasn't cursed, she was just set in the violent Pacific Ocean a mile from shore. Keepers were rotated every six weeks because conditions were so difficult. Lighthouse log books tell of crew members who passed notes at suppertime because they were no longer on speaking terms. Several keepers had to be removed because they seemed to have gone mad.

Stories about Terrible Tilly fascinated newspaper readers all over the country. Like the four-day winter storm in 1934 that blew boulders in waves 133 feet high. They crashed into the lantern room and cracked the lens. Waves also tore out the phone lines.

The keeper, an amateur radio operator, reported on their situation with a radio he made from waxed paper, tin foil, scavenged parts from the phone, and a brass doorknob. Even in the internet era the stories cause shivers—a website of strange and obscure places has a page titled, *Terrible Tilly, the Lighthouse of Death and Madness.*

Tilly was eventually decommissioned and her farewell toast was written in the lighthouse log book by her final keeper: *Farewell, Tillamook Rock Light Station. An era has ended. With this final entry, and not without sentiment, I return thee to the elements. You, one of the most notorious and yet fascinating of the sea-swept sentinels in the world; long the friend of the tempest-tossed mariner. Through howling gale, thick fog and driving rain your beacon has been a star of hope and your foghorn a voice of encouragement. May the elements of nature be kind to you.*

Tilly was sold to a series of private investors. For a while she served as the Eternity at Sea Columbarium. A New York Times article described this as *Terrible Tillie, Where the Departed Rest Not Quite in Peace.*

Now ships are warned off the dragon rock out in the waters by the mournful whistle buoy I'd heard.

I headed out in the morning, after my visit to say good-bye to Tilly, haunted by those low tones. The final two hour walk back to sea level followed a forestry road and dumped me just across the street from Wright's Campground, where I had made a reservation. There, behind the town of Cannon Beach, among old growth trees, I could still have been in the Tillamook Forest.

After a warm shower and lunch, I wandered out to find the town and the ocean. I'd gotten over worrying that anyone would covet my well-used pack or anything in my old, old nylon pup tent.

Cannon Beach was where Lewis and Clark had another misadventure on the Oregon Coast. They had thrown together a tiny one-room log cabin a little north, to shelter from the ever-falling rain. They called it, grandly, Fort Clatsop. They wintered there, miserable, hungry, crawling with lice and fleas. And enduring without rum, since there had been no four-master to meet them at the mouth of the Columbia.

One day a scout brought in a sample of blubber from a beached whale. Clark reported that it was good, *resembling the beaver or the dog in flavor.*

A group set out in canoes to buy or trade more of the delicacy. As they rounded Tillamook Head, they saw what Oregonians and tourists from around the world still flock to enjoy—in Clark's words: *inoumerable rocks of emence Sise out at a great distance from the Shore and against which the Seas brak with great force gives this Coast a most romantic appearance.*

But the whale was just a pile of bones by that time; an encampment of Chinook people had rendered most of the blubber into oil. As the explorers traded for oil to carry back, Clark's aide Hugh McNeal almost got his throat slit.

The way it's told in the local museum sounds like someone cleaned up the story. McNeal went to the Chinook camp across the river to trade one evening. A man wanted his blanket and attacked him. A woman who knew McNeal screamed. Someone fetched Clark, who rescued him.

Clark praised the Chinook woman in his journal, and wrote that the incident was an example of the great cooperation they enjoyed from the native peoples. However, he nicknamed the river where they were camped, "McNeal's Folly." The museum doesn't speculate how the Chinook woman had met McNeal. I got a chill when I researched further and found Clark's report that he treated McNeal with mercury for the clap six months later.

The town's name, Cannon Beach, came from another ship that wrecked in the Pacific near Astoria. The USS Shark struck the Columbia Bar in 1840 and one of her three cannons washed up down the beach.

A project to find the other two cannons from the Shark ended in 2008, when a teenager found two cannons in the sand further south. To me, the mystery isn't whether those cannons really came from the USS Shark, but how water, which has no shape of its own, has the power to lift and float cast iron; to throw boulders one hundred thirty-three feet high and break Tilly's lenses. How land and sea can separate and reconnect again and again with no emotion, no regret, no sorrow. How no matter how often Mark and I separated and reconnected, it was always so fraught.

Later, I walked into town to check on gas canisters (none). I still never thought to ask anyone about where I might find one. My learned self-reliance had gone on hyper-drive as I retreated inward to cope with lost routines and a loneliness that didn't seem likely to end.

I browsed along main street, now almost empty of tourists. In a high-tone store offering natural lotions and make-up, I moistened my dust-dried hands with a sample that smelled delicately of jasmine. A charming fountain sculpture stood across the street; a stack of slate stones arranged in the shape of a towering Douglas Fir with water tumbling down the layers. Such a romantic spot to write in my journal. But when I sat down on the low wall of the fountain, the buzzing pump drowned out the sound of trickling water.

If everything is a metaphor, as Trung had affirmed, this was a depressing one, how easily the grit of living drowns out the music. I got up quickly and walked back to camp.

I was on a pilgrimage to discover the opening that would lead out of my emotional pain and into my new future. At least, I hoped to get a vision of that future so I could orient myself. I was finding an interesting conversation between emotional and physical pain on the trail. I was discovering that beauty and metaphor lifted me above them both, but so temporarily. Does poetry work? Does beauty heal pain? Or are they part of each other forever, like dark and light?

I learned later that Thomas Jefferson set Meriwether Lewis up as governor of Louisiana Territory after he got back from Oregon. He fell into one of his deep depressions and never recovered the joy he'd experienced on the trail. He found the trials of exploring—of lice and fleas, hunger and rain—more tolerable than those of administrating. He drank and gambled. He couldn't get the scientific and geographic report of their explorations finished. Some bureaucrats began to question purchases he'd made for the trip and he feared bankruptcy. He finally set out for Washington to defend himself.

Only three years after their celebrated return from the Pacific Northwest, at age 35, Lewis was either murdered or killed himself in Tennessee, at a tavern along the Natchez Trace. He must have hoped he would walk home from the Pacific Ocean a different person.

Chapter 10

I went to bed with the light in Cannon Beach. Mark and I had usually gone to bed together. Even a year without him hadn't made sleeping alone easier. Just before dropping into sleep, I woke back up in tears.

Crying is in my DNA. My sisters and brother and I tear up as though our sweat glands are connected to our eyes. Our dad was the worst of us all. Dad cried reading tender Bible passages. He cried preaching. He cried when he spanked us.

I was used to crying when anything touched the Irish harp in my chest. But Mark's cancer had shot me into a prolonged state of tearfulness that I was hoping to walk my way out of. Instead, beginning in Cannon Beach, I cried in the forests. I cried in my tent. I cried at the picnic table. I cried among the trees. I cried among the indifferent sea gulls and the busy sand pipers. Tears ran down my face and my chin and down my neck. My nose dripped, as I searched in every pocket for a shred of TP tucked away somewhere. Instead of making me tougher, the trail scraped me raw.

Over the years, Mark figured out how to be kind about my tears and to understand that they would pass, he didn't need to freak out. Usually, he hit the balance pretty well. But during his episodes of depression and anger, he didn't care if I came or went. He didn't care what I wanted or needed. He didn't care if I cried. When my rugged, larger-than-life dad was felled by his glioblastoma brain tumor, Mark's depression lasted for several years.

I'd had a close but complicated relationship with Dad. With his brain tumor diagnosis, my siblings and I went into shock, circling around him, sharing his chemo and radiation trips among ourselves as though with our care we could ward off what we feared was coming. I was panicked. I couldn't bear to be separated from my first family, even fifty miles away on the farm in Salem.

After Dad died, Mark withdrew into a mixture of grief and anger for days at a time. I was too unbalanced to help Mark, too confused by my own mixture of sadness with guilt over unexpected relief—I didn't have to try so hard to please Dad anymore.

I cooked for Mark and me, we ate a sit-down supper together, he cleaned up—we were good at our routines even when we couldn't look at each other. We often sat together in the hot tub on our deck in the late evening, only together physically.

After months of this, I insisted he find someone to talk to. On one of our hot tub evenings, I slipped out of my seat on one side and went to sit beside him. I never could outwait him. It was a complicated dance, my hope, his fear. He could wallow in a panic about being abandoned as long as I was there and he stayed mad. And he could stay mad for a long time. I didn't touch him that evening, I just sat beside him. But he wasn't ready even for that.

"My counselor says you have a pathological need for closeness," he said.

I laughed. "That's pretty unprofessional. She's never even met me."

"She didn't say it exactly that way."

"What did she say? Exactly?"

"That your need for closeness is equal to my need for protection."

Wow. Was Mark trying to share some new self-knowledge? But he'd shot the message on an arrow that was barbed and poisoned. I was angry now. No longer in the mood for repair. "Did she say your need for protection was pathological?"

Mark didn't answer. Why did he want to damage the only closeness he had any access to?

And what about my pathological need for closeness? Or PNC Syndrome, as I called it when I told my sisters. Now that Mark was gone, I was forced to see just how needy I was.

I rolled over in my sleeping bag. My air mattress crackled as I groped around for a tissue. The wind shifted, blowing through the campground, and suddenly it sounded like Highway 101 was roaring right through. I could hear neighbors playing a guitar and singing, which I enjoyed until their campfire smoke drifted into my tent.

I buried my face in nylon and down until I dozed off. I woke again at midnight. The camp had fallen quiet and the moon looked down on me with silvery calm.

The next day, on a side street near the campground, I found the true treasures of town: the Cannon Beach Book Company and the Chocolate Cafe. I shyly told the bookstore owner about my walk, and asked for a recommendation.

He blushed as his face lit up. He pointed to *Trask* by Don Berry, and said it should have been a better-known book. "You'll be walking exactly the part of the beach where it takes place, past Arch Cape and down to Tillamook."

I scanned the introduction, which claimed the book is better than *Sometimes a Great Notion* by Ken Kesey. *One that has more to do with who we are as Oregonians and how we came so far in such a short time and lost so much along the way.* I bought it, thrilled that there was such a book, and amazed at another synchronicity that had brought me to this bookstore in this town on this hike, where two shy people had smiled at each other over our shared love for books, for knowledge, for Oregon.

"Thank you for walking," he said.

In the café, I ordered a chocolate crème caramel and a latte. *Trask* starts off with a quote from an Oregonian's journal in the 1840s: *I hear today from a Clackamas Indian there is some 'Dam Fool' of a white man has got himself into trouble with the Killamooks down at the coast, which have a pretty hard reputation. And who shd it turn out to be but my old Comrade Elbridge Trask that I free-trapped with out of Fort Hall. Well I am not surprised any but hope he does not get himself killd which wd be just like him. He was the most restless man I ever knew.*

I read on, carving tiny bites off the face of the crème caramel, eating my mousse like a mouse, as a friend had once observed.

That evening, a young couple, heading into town for supper, brought their camp light over to my campsite. I sat at the picnic table, warmed by the generosity of strangers. I nattered on in my notebook because I wasn't ready for bed and I had the luxury of light.

I wrote about the men I'd dated. My PNC pushed me toward romance. Loyalty to Mark and impatience with the shallows at the edges of new relationships pushed back. How would I get to know anyone well enough to know we were a match? No one is a heartthrob at age sixty-five.

My kids seemed nervous about someone new coming into the family. Jesse told me he and Kenny had talked. "We agreed we'll try to accept him for your sake," he said. "But the minute he calls me 'Son,' it'll be all over."

When the couple came back, I returned their lamp.

They were building up a little campfire. "Join us!"

They were Christians, they said, struggling with a decision about where to live. I hid my irritation at the conservative Protestant claim that God has a secret plan for us that He (or She?) doesn't divulge. We're supposed to discern that plan through prayer and little internal nudges of the Holy Spirit. Nudges are like newborns' facial expressions—*It's a smile! Or is it gas?*

I told them not to worry about God's will for where they live. The Bible makes it clear how to make moral and ethical decisions, but God expects us do our best thinking about practical decisions. There's no promise that there's a perfect plan for our lives, I said. Only, *Fear not*. That God will be with us in whatever future evolves from our decisions.

I guess they saw me as an older, wiser woman. They listened, nodding and staring into the flames, or maybe they just understood that I'm one of those mainline not-quite-Christians and they knew God really did have a perfect plan for their lives.

My tent the next morning, as I rolled it up, puffed stale campfire smoke into my face. I said good-bye to my neighbors and left the campground by nine. At the top end of the Cannon Beach boardwalk, I passed a bronze statue commemorating the whale whose blubber had been so delicious. And there, to my left, spread the wide cream-colored beach in bright sunlight. Haystack Rock, queen of Oregon's lava rock formations, serene and wild, stood over her own wavery reflection; a monolith shaped by the millennia, silhouetted against a sapphire sky, surrounded by her guards, the Needles. Peaceful and immovable, she was framed by the headland. The ocean broke and swirled at her feet.

Thousands of photos, taken in every light and from every angle, don't capture her majesty—the towering, sparkling basalt that was once liquid; the headlands behind her, draped in shades of green that turn blue and purple in the distance; the ocean, reflecting light back in moving, shimmering swells, wearing down the rock.

It was a beach-walk day again. Early sunlight and shadows played across heaving waves. The tide left silver washes of water behind on the wide, flat beach. We marvel at the ocean, but most of us stay on the edges. The depths of it we fear.

Over ten million years ago, lava had rolled in from fissures on the Oregon-Washington-Idaho border, some of it moving so fast it got to the Pacific Ocean in a week, still liquid. Geologists believe some of it spilled into the opening of an undersea volcano and spewed back up as Haystack Rock, the third tallest basalt stack in the world.

Over six hundred lava eruptions flooded Central Oregon and flowed into what geologists call the Columbia Basin, edging the original river further and further north. Soil now covers most of the lava fields, except where the Missoula Floods, carrying glacial ice, water and boulders, scoured soil away and exposed the many layers of lava that make the Columbia Gorge so dramatic.

Tufted puffins nest on Haystack Rock in the fall. On the day I was there, tape and cones protected the birds from curious tourists who clustered on the beach with binoculars. Close up, Haystack Rock looked more like a crime scene than the most photographed spot in Oregon.

I stepped off the boardwalk and turned to look north at Tillamook Head again. It stands high over town, the yew and hemlock on its steep sides dark in the shadows of morning. Tilly is sometimes just visible beyond Haystack Rock and the Needles, but people drive from Cannon Beach to Ecola State Park, a few miles north, if they want to see Tilly from sea level. The best views of Tilly are the ones I'd seen, evening and morning, from the lookout above.

Then I walked south, toward Arch Cape, where I would meet John Markham and his couch. One of the many creeks that flow out of the Coast Range and run under Highway 101 in culverts fanned out across the beach in front of me. It looked deeper than most. If I bent over to untie my boots with my pack on, I would tip right over on my head. The REI saleswoman had told me my boots were waterproof; why not find out?

I stepped in and stood at the shallow edge, waiting for an invading trickle. Nothing. I strode on across. But I had underestimated how the deeper water would push and mound up against me. Cold water poured in the tops of my boots and I lumbered quickly to the other side, laughing—every waterproof boot has a hole at the top.

The beach stretched for a couple miles, swept clean of driftwood, golden, with glistening reflections of sky on wet sand. But several points lay ahead, rocky bits of ancient lava that stand or lie along the tideline. Silver Point is surrounded with a litter of smaller lava rocks, with Jockey Cap Rock a sea arch in the making. The waves are grinding at it in foamy beauty, minute by minute.

Rocks change slowly, and so do our preferences, our personalities, our understanding. I was still haunted by the missing presence of Mark that I'd felt in bed the night before. I thought of how loyal he'd been in spite of his volatility. How he'd always been afraid I'd leave him. How ironic that in the end, he was the one to leave.

A line came back to me from a song my sister and I had sung with our guitars in college: Buffy Sainte-Marie promising to stay—until it was time for her to go. It took me three times through, humming the blank spots, before all the words came back. When I remembered the last line, that she might never see her love again, my tears fractured the sunlight and turned the sea and the beach into a kaleidoscope of muted blues and tan.

I wove my way through the sentinel rocks of Humbug Point. The pounding waves had crumbled some of the stone, but the bits still felt solid underfoot. Geologic crumbling could go on for eons. My life was an instant, and the crumbling of it evanescent.

I came to Hug Point, a blob of buried lava about five feet high, that sprawled over the beach. Sometimes at low tide, hikers can creep around the tip in the squishy sand. Bonnie Henderson had, of course. But there was a high low tide that day, thigh-deep. The surging waves might lift me off my feet. A narrow road had been chiseled into the rock, first for stage coaches and then for cars, Bonnie said. I clambered up, saying *sorry, sorry, sorry* to tiny white barnacle-like creatures that encrusted the rock and crunched underfoot.

On the other side, a log-littered beach led to Falcon Head and the ocean-carved stone that Arch Cape is named for. The town was not far, but John Markham wasn't expecting me until after four. It was high noon when I got to where cabins poked up behind the low sea grass. I had a long afternoon to spend on the beach. I found a log to lean back against and hitched my wide-brimmed hat low over my face to protect it. Gusts whipped sand up into my face. Rather than take the risk of unwrapping my cheese, I squeezed almond butter furtively out of a packet and onto my crackers, trying to shelter them from the blowing sand with my shoulder.

That afternoon I was completely happy. Singing had brought a prick of pain, and had also lit up my brain. The clean smell of salt, waves shushing on the beach in the background, the rocky vistas and the easy beach walking left me at ease, able to rest from my chronic thrum of anxiety.

I had spent too much time imagining a future full of shadows and loneliness, letting fear of my unknown new life shade my mood. Every couple in a long marriage must wonder, Will I leave or be left? And which is more bearable? The first question had been answered now. The second I would never know.

My son-in-law had said they believed in me, that I would thrive again and be happy. Miriam added, "Can you imagine the shape Dad would have been in about now, if he were alone?" She shuddered.

I opened *Trask*, tipped my head so the shadow of it sheltered the bright page, and read about this restless white man, who pierced the geographical defenses of the Tillamook (or Killamook) people. Until then, their coves and meadows had been protected from invading settlers by rivers and the rugged headlands. The Tillamook had watched other peoples like the Chinook be decimated by white men's drink and diseases. They had fiercely guarded their fortresses. *Trask* is about inevitability, the better of bad options, and prices paid. I lay back against the log and slept.

I was sandy and aching by the time I roused. There was no longer any way, at my age, to sit comfortably on the ground for hours. I had to either stretch my legs out straight until my hamstrings complained, or sit cross-legged and shift the pain to my hips.

I stood stiffly and hoisted the pack off the ground. The sun was dropping, sunlight shifting from bright yellow to thick gold. I set off again, down the beach, to look for John Markam's house. He'd told me he would have a flag up. And there it was, on a sandy knoll in the lee of Cape Falcon, its rope snapping against the flagpole.

Chapter 11

John met me at the back door dressed in rumpled khaki and flannel. His face was pleasantly wrinkled. My pack towered over me and crowded the small kitchen. When John finished a few awkward words of welcome, he led me to a bedroom. He limped.

The room smelled old, of dust and wallpaper glue. A vintage silver hand mirror and hairbrush lay on the low dressing table, their images reflected in hinged mirrors. Dust dimmed the mirrors and the silver looked dull gray. A sewing machine stood open. A multitude of spools of thread lay jumbled in a box, their colors muted by dust. The photos on the wall stretched back at least three generations.

John showed me where to turn the shut-off valve in the ensuite bathroom when I needed water. "Otherwise, the toilet runs," he said. He turned back to the bedroom. "I'll let you make up the bed. Sheets are there. That one, I rescued out of someone's garbage."

I shook out the sheets and made up the nearest of the twin beds. The sheet with a big patch, I put on top. There was an interesting lacy gray design all over it. Then I realized the design was the roots, branches, tendrils of a well matured mildew garden. I leaned down and sniffed. Whatever near-death experience that sheet had been through, now it smelled only of laundry detergent.

I took off my shoes and rubbed the sand from between my toes into the toilet, put on a clean t-shirt, and reported for supper duty. Worn linoleum demarcated the kitchen and dining area, dominated by an antique table under huge windows overlooking the sea.

Through an arch to the side sat an old couch, a recliner imprinted with the shape of John's body, and end tables piled with papers. Dozens of carved and fired elephants marched across the mantle of a fireplace.

"My mother collected them," John said, when he saw me looking. "I used to travel and I brought them to her from all over the world." John had taken care of his mom in that house until her death.

The stove hood hadn't been wiped down any more recently than the bedroom. A cast iron skillet smelled of bacon grease and still had bits of potato skin clinging to the sides. John was clearly a member of the family that had bred my mom, with her sign welcoming spiders to the kitchen. He opened the basement door to get apples and potatoes. As he started down, I saw that his limp was more than a slight difficulty.

I went to wash my hands before starting, and turned the water quickly back off at the sound of it splashing below the sink. John had a bucket to catch the gray water, and an empty for when it got full. I took a deep breath, rinsed out the frying pan, and cooked up supper.

He did most of the talking over our meal. He was a Stanford grad, a retired marine biologist. He still took the temperature of the ocean morning and evening for his research; wrote articles for scientific journals; did deep sea dives around the world. He also jogged every morning, before sunrise. "My legs don't work right. I run like a caterpillar. I don't want my neighbors to have to watch me so I run in the dark."

"What happened to your legs?"

"A car accident. A seizure. I should have died. A kid on a bike saw my car down off the road and called 911. I woke up in traction in ICU in Portland. They had put me back together like a jigsaw puzzle."

We sat facing the ocean, watching the sun go down. The big picture window had lost its seal and was blurry with moisture, but that just made the sunset's brilliant refraction of every shade of yellow, orange, and red more interesting. Mottled clouds shaded the colors with gray. Heaving waves broke up the reflections, lined them with silver, sent them flashing in every direction. If I tipped my head a little to the left, I could see the huge orange sun precisely etched through a clear spot. One tiny ship's light gleamed silver on the horizon.

John's father had been the first in the neighborhood to weatherize his house. He'd ordered the double-glazed windows from Chicago and they'd come by train, back when such a thing was unheard of.

John invited me to stay for breakfast and described his morning routine. He would put nine grain cereal into water, turn on the water heater, and go out in the dark for his run. When he got back, the water would be hot for his shower. By the time he finished, the cereal would be ready to go. He would cook it, using a minimum of gas. He'd turn the water heater off and let warm water coast all day.

Later, I fell asleep wondering whether I'd ever have as much heart as John Markham, a brilliant man who'd lost much, but went on to live his quirky and frugal life on the beach alone. I was frugal, but not that frugal. I was smart, but not that smart. I'd be alone, but would I be that much alone?. I hoped my interests would also sustain me.

I woke with the light and thought about my next long hike, over ten miles. For that night, I had reserved a room in a motel in the town of Manzanita, on the other side of Falcon Head. After our breakfast, John said he'd show me the trailhead.

I hated to make him labor over the uneven ground, but he insisted. He had to walk to the post office anyway, he would drop me at the rope bridge over the creek. "The fir and hemlock have different elevation preferences," he told me. "See if you can tell. The line between them is pretty distinct."

As we said good-bye, I invited him to Portland if he ever needed a couch to crash on. Three months later he would take me up on it, and would come to town for his dive-club's Christmas party. He would write again the following year and tell me about several dives and the meeting of the International Crustacea Society at the Australian Museum. He had brought the Museum's collection of isopods back to Oregon to work up. Most of the collection had been his own donated samples.

As I crossed the creek and started up the path, a song came back that had been singing in my head as I woke up in John's mother's bedroom. A song about loss.

Mark and I had set out hopefully together, having found each other again in college when we were twenty. It was the early 70s and jobs were easy to find, but the adult world still gave us a hard, hard time. My first job, teaching in a Chicago Catholic girls' school, went terribly wrong. The next year, Mark moved us to a western Minnesota farm. But there my depression deepened. I sat alone all day on what was still called the Jacobson Place, with nothing to do but cook Mark's meals. Town women my age had several children but no college. I mostly had contact with older women on these farms. They were also alone all day, oozing discontent. As I did, they cooked and did for their overwhelmed farmer husbands.

Mark's farming dream turned into a march of endurance when the herbicide failed. He spent dawn to dark on hot summer days with a crew that whacked pigweed out by hand in the soybean fields. Mark came in for lunch starving, covered in dust, blisters bleeding.

When summer mercifully ended and the winter lull set in, the Jacobson Place burned to ashes with all of our earthly possessions. We didn't have many, but what we had were more than just things: Mark's complete collections of Beatles and Gordon Lightfoot music on reels of tape; my animal carvings from Kenya; posters of Ethiopia; the Hummel cellist figurine that Mom had given me when I took up the cello in high school.

After the fire, we'd gone back to Chicago and started over.

Now, on the OCT, I needed to start over again. I was listening only to my own desires. But my desires were interrupted and rattled by memories, those strange bursts of energy in the brain that persist even as the cells that generate them are replaced. Tear bursts in response to the memories, which only lasted until both evaporated and I was left in the quiet forests again, or by the ocean that never tired, never rested.

As I walked away from John Markham's house in Arch Cape, I thought maybe I really could manage a long new life alone. His heroism made adjusting to a normal life alone seem feasible.

But the climb up Falcon Head was grueling. My confidence leaked away. Over and over, I looked above me and saw only a tangle of underbrush. What would I do, lacking a machete, if the path had gotten overgrown? Again and again, at the last minute, the path switched sharply back. The way forward showed up, narrow, but clear, just in time. I was too tired to appreciate the metaphor. All day I asked myself, *Is there a way forward?* There always was. Over and over, I asked, exhausted, *Can I do this? Can I do it alone?* Apparently, I could.

Besides the switchbacks, the climb involved turn-offs, and spurs, and poorly signed crossings. Every transition left me anxious. In one case, I turned the wrong way, toward the ocean from about sixteen hundred feet high. I found myself going down a steep incline through waist-high brush. I kept going too long. When I finally turned, scrambling back up, my heart was pounding. I felt endangered. The weight of the pack was pulling me back down a slope that probably ended at the edge of a cliff.

Finally, the trail leveled. My breath eased. I wound through hemlock and cedar and spruce; sword fern grew thick on the forest floor. The trail then rose again into older fir woods, where the cedar fell away and deer fern, salal and red huckleberries formed a twiggy understory. Then it climbed up into another rainforest, where the duff rotted sweetly into earth and smelled of fern fronds. Roots crisscrossed the path and held geometric puddles.

The stillness was deep at the top of Falcon Head. At eye level I was surrounded by a thousand rough tree trunks. I stopped to look up, up into the mass of dark green needles high above me. They blocked out the sky. They swayed in a breeze that didn't reach the ground. I felt sheltered. No matter what wild storm might shake this high forest, it would always return to calm, to regeneration, to growth.

That forest thinned and the path started up another set of switchbacks, into a thick stand of young alder. Through their skinny trunks I could see uphill to Highway 101, hugging the side of the bluff. Below me, the cliff dropped to the silent dreamy ocean.

Further on, I paused at a fork, studying Bonnie Henderson's instructions. I turned uncertainly onto an old logging road hemmed in by the young alders. It felt like the wrong direction. But the wrong way exiting restaurants and hotel rooms always felt right to me, so what felt wrong should be right. And it was. The path delivered me, as Bonnie promised it would, onto the shoulder of Highway 101. I stood for a long time, contemplating the crossing between cars and RVs that whipped by. I felt more like a turtle than a creature that could dash.

This was my first experience with the most frustrating feature of the OCT: in some places there is no way for a trail to squeeze between the ocean and the headlands. There is no choice other than to walk on the graveled shoulder of a narrow two-lane highway. I call it a shoulder, but in places, it is no wider than a footpath.

Finally, I came to the trail opening into the other side of the alder forest, thick but full of green and yellow light.

Somewhere along the way, I had passed from Clatsop County into Tillamook County. My pedometer suggested I should soon be in Manzanita. But the trail went on and on. The uneven path seemed particularly narrow. I lurched and tipped; the pack unbalanced me, as I got more and more exhausted. *You are an unsafe hiker,* I told myself. *Slow down.* I took out the whistle a friend had given me, in case I toppled into a thicket of ferns. But who would hear my whistle and come to help me up?

The blog said a person might bivouac on Cape Falcon. I checked my water bottle. I looked for a level spot where a tiny tent, no longer than six feet, no wider than four, would fit. But this forest was thick with new growth. I trudged on. The path wound up and up, toward the highway again. When would I get up to the road, and how could I possibly manage several more miles on hard-packed gravel when I got there?

My feet ached, the bone-deep ache that always set in soon after the eighth mile. All those bones in my feet—every one of them hurt.

They had flexed a million times that day, cradled in their web of muscles and ligaments.

The path finally dead-ended at the rocky base of the roadbed. I had to climb over the metal barrier. And I was on a curve. What a rag-tag trail it was, this OCT.

Turn right on the spur off to the town of Manzanita, Bonnie wrote. The highway was quiet as I set out on its narrow edge. I sent a breath of thanks for that, and added, *If you ever want to send me a ride, this would be the time.*

Historic markers ringed the half circle of a turn-out ahead. Tired as I was, walking the turn-out would get me off the shoulder and distract my suffering mind with something new to learn. I stumbled over to the first brass marker. An old faded turquoise station wagon pulled in. A man leaned over and shouted out the passenger window. "Can I give you a ride?"

I didn't have the energy to speak, barely to nod and smile.

Santa Claus, with a pure white beard and a belly, stepped out of the car. I thought I might be hallucinating. He opened the hatch-back and pushed aside bales of toilet paper to make room for my pack.

People with nefarious intentions don't look like Santa and hoard toilet paper. And anyway, hadn't I asked for him?

God doesn't intervene in the details of our lives; I'd said it so firmly to the couple in Cannon Beach. But when I reached the end of my strength, sure enough, like the atheist in the foxhole, I'd cried out, *Dear God...!*

Anne Lamot says that there are really only three prayers: *Wow, help,* and *thanks.* I'd been praying *Wow* as often as I could. Now I prayed *Thank you* all the way down the hill to Manzanita.

And *Help?* Maybe the prayer itself opens us to help that is all around us, or about to show up. Santa said he would be driving right by the motel where I had reserved a room.

I nodded. Nothing was going to surprise me.

"I run the Winery at Manzanita," he said. Which explained all the TP. Limp against the seat back and headrest, I wasn't sure I would be able to hold myself up when it was time to get out.

The motel was a crummy dive. Better than my pup tent, but a dive that cost a hundred dollars because it was on the coast. I stumped into the bathroom and hung my crumpled silk tank on a hook to loosen the wrinkles in a steamy shower. *Sorry feet*—there was no tub for the soaking I'd promised them.

I had looked up a restaurant in town, but from the doorway of my room I could see a tasteful neon sign, *Big Wave Café*. It was going to be expensive by the look of the low, subtly-lit building, the golden pine siding and tasteful landscaping. I wasn't sure I could walk even that far. But for a hot meal, I would try.

At the café, I ordered salmon and bulgur. I chewed slowly. The lighting was dim, the music low. Tears of gratitude for help, for hot food, for the coming night in a bed, flooded my eyes.

By the next day, as always, my feet were fine. A few years later, I wrecked the joint in the ball of my right foot digging sod out of my new front yard in Portland. For a week I really did limp, and after that I could only dance for about an hour before my foot hurt too much to go on.

"It's congenital," the podiatrist said, completely discounting the sod-digging. "It's because of the angle of your knees and ankles. Custom orthotics will help." I shuddered—how would I dance in old-lady shoes with orthotics? But then she said, "We'll get you hiking again."

So now I assume that my genes were at fault for the way my feet hurt walking the OCT. I marvel that I never considered abandoning the hike because of my pain. Maybe pushing on through the pain was the real metaphor of my pilgrimage, one that I didn't think about at the time. And it's classic. Lots of us look for physical pain to distract us from emotional pain, and then, unappreciative and barely aware of what we're doing, we grudge the physical.

Chapter 12

Low tide in Manzanita was around noon the next day, so I relaxed over my breakfast of leftover bulgar and salmon. I sat all morning at a tiny table under the window looking out to the street, and wrote in my journal. At noon, I packed up quickly, so practiced by this time, and walked down the street to look for lunch. Oregon coast towns are narrow, most of them dropped between the sand and the cliffs. Manzanita was about two blocks wide. At the end of my street, I could see the teal and blue ocean meeting pale sand.

I got a fat sandwich wrapped in brown butcher paper at a grocery deli. Further down the street, I ducked on impulse into an ice cream shop and walked back out with a cone piled high with Tillamook Dairy's pralines and cream. At a bench on a wooden platform at the edge of the sand, I set the sandwich down and wiggled carefully, one-handed, out of the pack. I propped my legless companion beside me.

Then I stared at the cone. I was going to have to eat my dessert first. Had I ever done that before?

The day ahead was supposed to hold a new adventure. No big climb, but a flat walk and something Bonnie Henderson described this way: *One of the best things about hiking the OCT, in my opinion, is catching boat rides across the bay mouths. This first one is the easiest; just wave your arms at the end of Nehalem Spit and, like magic, a boat appears.*

Or, she promised that a passing speedboat would swing in to pick me up. That was the way to avoid having to walk the highway around the bay.

My first three miles in Nehalem State Park delighted me, with a beach breeze off the ocean in the warming air and the company of my new self who would eat ice cream first. A person who was freer. More light-hearted.

Delight lasted until I had to leave the packed low-tide sand and walk across the spit. I was supposed to follow a horse trail. The loose sand was deep. It shifted under my feet and slipped away when I pushed off the next step. Seagrass, waist high, nodded over the sand and slashed against my legs below my nylon hiking skirt. Instead of the ocean scents, the forest scents, there was only the smell of dry grass and dust and horse.

The spit went on forever. Spurs branched off the path everywhere. I kept choosing to go in the direction I thought was east, to the mainland side of the spit, but I worried more and more that I could be lost. I couldn't camp in the endless seagrass—my water wouldn't hold out. I didn't dare let my mind wander into metaphors. If my life as a widow was going to be a slog in loose sand and slashing sea-grass, I didn't want to know.

I finally broke out on the edge of a bluff. Between me and the still, green bay were gray boulders as big as recliners and coffee tables. Across the water, as promised, the marina.

I let myself down, balancing carefully with my top-heavy pack, afraid of breaking a leg on the rocks. I jumped down the last boulder, safely onto the sand, and stumbled under the jolt of the extra weight. I started down the beach, waving to the marina. A cluster of stones on the edge of the water suddenly flipped and flopped into the bay—sea lions that had lain utterly still, sunning themselves.

Based on what Bonnie Henderson had written, I thought I'd be waving to someone working out on the dock. But I was looking at the back of the marina. It was closed up tight. Bay water lapped at my brown boots. I waved again, but then stopped, feeling silly. No one was there. I turned on my phone, since Bonnie had also supplied the marina's number. No service.

I sat down on the sand. Sweat prickled around my hairline under my floppy nylon hat in the early afternoon sun. My mind slowed down and stopped. I had no options, no metaphors, no melodies or harmonies with heart-touching words. I had the bay and about a cup of water.

A motorboat buzzed along, a sleek white one with shiny chrome. I jumped up. I waved madly. The pilot sent me his *No way!* response in an arc of spray that sparkled in the sunshine. Maybe those wealthy motorboat men would have swung in for the long-legged, 28-year-old, gorgeous-even-when-camping Bonnie of my imagination. But they weren't going to waste their time rescuing me, a scruffy older woman with a pack, out on a spit alone.

I sipped a bit of water, but only a bit, in case I was stuck there for the night. Lying back in the sand, against the one stone that had not been a sea lion, I closed my eyes. Maybe my discouragement was mostly a sugar low from the delicious, indulgent ice cream. I smiled at that, probed for regret, and found none.

After a couple of hot and drowsy hours, action broke out on the deck across the bay. A crowd gathered around a small flotilla of row boats. This was a private group of some sort. I watched, too embarrassed to wave, but hopeful there'd be someone left to rescue me once they set sail.

Heading my way, voices and laughter echoed across the water. A party. But behind them, the marina shut tight again. The row boats pulled in down from me. No one looked my way. I forced myself to stand up. We don't get the help we want; we get the help we get.

Chapter 13

I walked, drowning in shame, toward the picnickers on the beach. They were going to lean away from me. They'd think I was an old woman who would ruin their party by chattering cliches and trying to show them pictures of her grandchildren. They would think of their own eccentric grandmother. They didn't know how to talk to her, and avoided being in the same room with her alone.

Who was Bonnie Henderson, that she could enjoy this? Maybe Bonnie was funny, bubbly, and outgoing as well as tall and beautiful. Maybe she could have shouted and waved the minute she saw the group on the dock. Maybe she could have welcomed them like a reigning queen onto her spit, instead of cringing, in hiking boots and a skirt, in a grubby t-shirt, with a floppy hat shading my sweaty face, hiding sweaty bangs and a graying ponytail. One thing I knew, she wouldn't have been three times as old as these young people, my only hope of not spending the night with the sea lions.

I smiled the warmest smile my stiff lips could manage. I asked a young woman if I could get a ride across when they went back. Everyone stopped chattering and turned to look.

She looked around uncomfortably. "Do we have room?" The skinny guy beside her made a show of counting people and seats. I have to call them kids. I couldn't see faces, through my blinding embarrassment, only a sea of t-shirts, flowing hair, and bare, toned legs.

"Do you have a life jacket?" the guy asked.

Dumbfounded, but too desperate to make a joke, I just said, "I'm hiking."

There was a long pause. Everyone looked at the guy. Then he nodded.

I retreated to my sea lion rock up the beach. The hot shame drained out slowly. I took a deep breath. The kids had turned their backs again and were getting on with their party, but I thought their laughter sounded more subdued. The plight of a stranger doesn't belong at a picnic.

Elbow on my knee, I stared at the sand and waited. As the shame faded, fear rose, like the rise of the water at my feet as the tide came up. The randomness of my rescue! The young people could have come some other day! Hours before! To a different beach! They could have said no. I struggled to breathe. I couldn't feel my gratitude.

By the time I climbed into the boat with the girl and the skinny guy, I was numb. My pack made me top-heavy and awkward. The boat rocked crazily. I had already made such a fuss, I couldn't make more trying to wrestle the pack off on the narrow seat. I sat frozen. My fear of making these strangers more annoyed ran deeper than my will to live. The pack would just have to drown me if we tipped.

The girl offered me a sandwich, some fruit, and a smile. "We have a ton of leftovers."

The sandwich was bulging with egg or tuna salad and the fruit glistened with moisture for my dry throat. I just sat, holding them on my lap. Eating might tip the boat and I would die. I spoke through tight, chapped lips. "Thank you. Who are y'all?"

They were on a team-building day at the coast, she said; the entire staff of a Mexican restaurant called Porque No? on Mississippi Avenue in North Portland. Did I know the place? *Porque no?*

Porque there are a lot of eateries tucked in among the boutiques on Mississippi, a street of warehouses turned chichi. I didn't eat at any of them, being alone. But I didn't explain. Just smiled back, with the trickle of gratitude that was returning as we neared the dock.

I got out of the boat as quickly as I dared. None of us said goodbye to each other. I glanced at the menu sandwich board in front of the marina, but kept going, up toward the highway, beyond the stony seawall where the brown water of the bay lapped, full of debris, away from the cursed spit and my intense embarrassment.

I was headed for Highway 101 again, but I paused when I came to the railroad tracks. I was pretty sure the train didn't run any more. It wasn't easy walking. The rocky rail bed was hard on my feet and the ties were too far apart for my stride. But it felt so much better than deep, loose sand, safer than Highway 101. I felt a surge of relief, another *Thank you*. Like the Zen master who told his followers, *Meditate on your non-toothache*, I was meditating on my non-drowning. In the dappled sunlight, even the smell of tar and creosote seemed interesting, inoffensive.

But after I dropped back down to Rockaway Beach, the sand-trudge went on and on. Before long, the shushing waves, the gulls, sun on the sand and water were just so much static. The day had been more than I could bear.

When I got to the turn-off, a sign informed me that the Barview Jetty County Campground was another mile inland. I wanted to cry.

I dropped my pack at the first tent site I came to, a shadeless, featureless place with a worn picnic bench. I hobbled to the restroom. My pedometer said I'd walked seventeen miles. I knew my stride was shorter than the pedometer robot thought. Okay, fifteen miles.

Sometimes we really have no choice but to endure. There are many levels of suffering, but endurance is always numb misery, no hope, no thought of the future. Any energy has to be spent going on.

Both Mark and I had endured to his death. Even morphine hadn't extinguished his cancer pain. Near the end, he told me he was terrified of his organs shutting down. I asked the hospice nurse. She said organ shut-down pain is only when it happens suddenly. In a case like Mark's, it happens silently over time until life falls gently over the edge.

The heart is the only organ not affected by cancer, she said. It just keeps doing its best, delivering oxygen to the other organs for another day. And another.

Mark's parents were both still alive in their late eighties. Mark should have inherited old age. His heart kept going for weeks after he stopped eating. Hospice nurses who had gushed to me about the woman living for weeks just on Crystal Lite fell silent as Mark's fingernails continued to look pink and healthy, his oxygen levels stayed high, and the color of his feet was normal. They pulled aside the sheet to show me, but all I could see was his pale skin, almost transparent over the bones and tendons they no longer hid.

When she oriented us, the hospice nurse had said she'd come twice a week. She began to come every day. When I asked how long she thought Mark would continue to live—to drift, to hallucinate, to lose weight—she asked me what I thought. *You are the one who sees him hour by hour. Do you see changes?*

I was appalled to think I was the expert.

Mark asked me if he could go to the hospice hospital to die. He had spent a week there in August, to stabilize his pain. I wished with all my heart that they would take him back, his care had turned so hard. It had been a shock that hospice advises, medicates, offers comfort services like bathing, hair cuts, and massage. But day by day, it's family who cares for dying loved ones. We all want to die at home, surrounded by love, not tubes and flashing red lights. I wanted to give that gift to Mark. But by the beginning of October, when he wasn't eating but was living on, I was exhausted.

He'd lost the strength to walk to the bathroom before he lost the taboo for peeing as he lay there. No matter that I carefully arranged a diaper and a pad for that purpose. He would struggle for a half hour or longer in the night, trying to let down, while I got more desperately tired. I begged him. I snapped at him. I threatened to turn the light back off and let whatever was going to happen, happen without me.

When the nurse asked if he'd be willing to be catheterized, he thought about it, morphine-slow. He nodded. "It might save my marriage."

I laughed, and said to the nurse, "A man who will be catheterized to save his marriage is one in a million."

Emptying his catheter bag was now one of my jobs. I averted my eyes from the maroon sludge in the bottom. The nurse said it was debris from kidney cells being sloughed.

"I want to go back to the hospital," Mark said.

The hospice hospital had been lovely. A man had come and played the piano in the lobby several times a week. Someone went from room to room with a flute one day, serenading. But they used the few beds in that sweet little place for respite, to manage the exhaustion of the caretakers or the pain of the dying, not for dying itself.

I reminded Mark of the piercing pain he'd felt during the ambulance ride, strapped to a stiff hard gurney that pressed against the tumor next to his spine.

He closed his eyes, disappointed. "The bed was bigger there," he said.

I understood then. I'd spent most of every day with him there in the hospital. As Mark slept, I'd sat peacefully, looking out for hours at a water feature and the brass statues of deer and elk. When he was awake, I had often climbed into the bed with him and cuddled.

We say we want to die at home. We picture ourselves in comfy pajamas, drifting peacefully toward the edge, or maybe opening our eyes to see pure white light beckoning to us from across the River Styx. Only the luckiest of us get that death. And, someone we love has to care for us. Day and night, I was nurse to Mark now, not wife. I couldn't hold him.

He looked like those photos of starving Ethiopians. His skin was flaking. His mustache had grown and was curving over his top lip. His collarbone stood out like a yoke below his thin neck with its dozens of tendons. When I changed his Depends, I had to tip his bones and flesh up on one side, pleat and tuck the supplies in under him, tip him the other direction and pull them out straight. I had to be careful not to pinch his arm or the cord that connected him to the morphine pump. There were no soft pajamas. I could see the seams where the ball joints fit into his hip sockets. His body felt stiff and hard as a cadaver.

I took Mark's hand. He drifted back into his morphine haze. And I didn't have the energy yet to regret feelings of tenderness I wanted to feel but couldn't manage. We endured.

Chapter 14

At the Barview Jetty County Campground, around 5:30 the next morning, a breeze fluttered my rain fly. The light filtering in seemed strangely dim. I closed my eyes to doze a bit longer. Drops ticked on the tent. I smelled rain on dust.

The rain stopped after twenty minutes. I crawled out. Water had beaded up on the gray picnic table. My pack under the table was dry, but I'd left my bright purple cushion on the bench and water bubbled out when I pressed on it.

That day, I had to get around Tillamook Bay. The bay's rocky sea walls crowd so tightly that Highway 101 was slipped in only by blasting away some of the headland. I had already decided not to walk, but to take the bus. Now, on my schedule, I saw that the early bus passed the campground at 7:10. Maybe I could make it.

My sleeping bag and mat were wet where the tent sloped down at the bottom and touched my feet. I mashed them into my pack, hoping the bus would be running late—time to worry about wet gear later.

I walked quickly to the entrance of the campground, but there was nowhere to sit and wait by the road. A tiny convenience store was still closed. Piles of firewood sat beside the door. Wrappers littered the parking area. I rocked back and forth on my feet. Finally, I accepted that the first bus had not been running late. I set out for Garibaldi on foot after all, to catch the bus there.

A wall of black basalt rose up on one side of the road. I couldn't see the top. Its face, blasted into a thousand planes and angles, was wet and shiny. On the side where I was walking, the road-bed couldn't really be called a shoulder. It sloped away, gritty with fine black gravel that wanted to slip beneath my hiking boots. A vehicle roared up behind and scared me.

As soon as I could, I crossed to the cliff so I'd at least be facing traffic. The shoulder was more level there, but I could touch the basalt with one hand and hang the other out over the edge of the road. It curved, so there was still no warning of oncoming traffic. An RV rushed at me. I shrank against the wall as it passed. The side mirror whizzed by, only a couple of feet from my face. There just wasn't enough room between the bay and the rock. The OCT should be advertised as a Walk 'N Ride adventure.

When I saw picnic tables at the Tillamook Bay Wayside, I gladly crossed again and shed my pack. I pulled out my food bag for breakfast. As I ate granola, I read the big historic marker. The letters had been carved deep into a wooden panel topped by the carving of a beaver outlined in white paint.

This was a replacement sign, revised in 2013 to include the story of Markus Lopius, a black man in the crew of Captain Robert Gray's *Lady Washington*, which had put in at Tillamook Bay in 1788. Gray had added Lopius to the crew at an island off the coast of West Africa. They'd sailed around Cape Horn and along the coast of South America, trading along the way.

One day, after they dropped anchor in Tillamook Bay, half the crew of twelve traded otter pelts with Native peoples while the other half cut grass to feed the ship's meat supply, still on the hoof. Lopius was among the grass-cutters, and left his cutlass lying on the ground as he worked. When a young Native American took it, Lopius chased and caught him. The young man's friends attacked with knives and spears. Lopius tried to run back to safety, but they shot him with arrows. The rest of the crew dashed for the ship and put back out to sea. No one knows where Lopius was buried.

I researched the history on the Tillamook Bay Wayside sign when I got home. At its dedication, Gwen Carr, president of the Oregon Black Pioneers, said, "We are pleased that this important piece of Oregon's history has been added to the historical marker. It commemorates the earliest documented instance of a person of African descent being in Oregon, and serves as a memorial for those who came before and after, whose names and circumstances will never be known." Some historians think that Captain Drake's ship, also carrying crew members from Africa, may have put in at the bay near Manzanita in the 1750s.

Oregon went on to be the only state in the Union that disallowed slavery but banned African heritage people from settling. It was to have been a white utopia. An exclusionary law was passed in 1849 specifically to drive out black sailors who might jump ship and stay. Jacob Vanderpool did just that in 1850. Denied the right to own land, he had opened a tavern and general store. Some people defensively say that the exclusionary law was practiced only once, on Jacob Vanderpool.

But the exclusionary law stayed on the books even as both our senators and our one representative at the time voted in favor of the 13th amendment banning slavery in 1865.

The next year, Oregon ratified the 14th amendment, which extends all rights to all citizens and rendered the exclusionary law ineffective. But two years later, the legislature rescinded their ratification. It took Oregon ninety more years, until 1956, to ratify the 15th amendment allowing all citizens to vote. And only in 1973 did Oregon make its winding way back to re-ratify the 14th amendment.

In fact, amendment or no amendment, the people of Oregon voted in 1900 not to take the exclusionary law off the books. It remained until 1921. And only in 2022 did we Oregonians pass a ballot measure banning the racist language that permits *slavery and involuntary servitude* as punishment for crimes. Three of the other four states with similar votes that year were Alabama, Louisiana, and Tennessee. The Oregon State Sheriff's Association opposed removing that language, and half a million Oregonians followed its lead.

These facts of Oregon history are shocking to me, since I returned to Oregon as an adult who thought her state's liberal reputation was earned.

Oregon's white nationalist beginnings had meanwhile opened the way for discriminatory banking practices. In the black neighborhoods of North and Northeast Portland, they capped loans at one fourth to one sixth the size of loans in other parts of the city. Then, when people couldn't afford to repaint, repair, and reroof their homes, the city fathers called it urban blight and railed that it would spread and spoil Portland. They plowed Interstate-5 right through the middle of the neighborhood that black residents had been hemmed into. Under the guise of expanding Emmanuel Hospital, they destroyed what was left of a thriving *Little Harlem*. After black families were forced to sell their homes for pennies on the dollar and the neighborhood razed, the hospital expansion project went bankrupt.

Finally in 1990, *The Oregonian* ran a series called *Blueprint for a Slum*, and housing policies began to change. But that brought what is now pushing black families out of these historically diverse neighborhoods: gentrification. The rising cost of housing and property taxes is continuing the job of keeping Portland white.

With Intel and our position on the Pacific Rim, Oregon has citizens with Asian origins. An agricultural state, we have citizens and transient workers from Central America. And still, our diversity is pretty skimpy. When the Black Lives Matters demonstrations erupted in downtown Portland in 2020, Black activists from other places asked why the demonstrating crowds in Portland were so white. A Black Portlander said, *There are more Black Lives Matter signs in Portland than there are Black lives!*

My sisters and I had the reverse experience, growing up as the only white children in the surrounding Ethiopian community. But I wasn't oppressed for my skin color—there were no laws against my being there, as long as my parents had work permits. I was just stared at, my skin touched, my hair stroked curiously. That's a world away from systems that would limit my options, put me in danger (mortal or otherwise), and pound me emotionally with messages of less-than.

When my family settled again in North Portland in 1978, I hadn't heard of and couldn't immediately see the history of racist laws in ambivalently liberal Oregon. Sometimes now I'm overcome with guilt—I could afford to buy in spite of the rising housing costs. As a gentrifier in the whitest big city in the U.S, I'm part of the destruction of the very diversity I love in my neighborhood. I reassure myself that life is too complex for any of us to live with pristine hands. But the young hippie inside whispers, *That's a sell-out.*

So, I live across the street from a park. It's a place where no one stares and people of every shade of skin color seem to feel at home. Unless I'm still missing something.

At the Tillamook Bay Wayside, the morning sun rose above the trees and into my eyes. I ferried my granola bowl, my water, and my pack to the other table, still in shade.

When I finished and started off on the last mile into Garibaldi, I suddenly realized I wasn't wearing my glasses. I felt my head, my pockets, the front of my shirt where I sometimes hung them. Awkwardly, my pack heavily bumping, I ran back to the turnout. I looked on both tables. I looked on the benches.

Did I hook my glasses around a strap on the pack? I shifted it around and onto a table. I rifled through every pocket. Then I checked everything again: face, t-shirt, pockets, tables, pack.

Not even getting stuck on the end of the spit on Nehalem Bay panicked me as much as losing my glasses. I didn't much need them for distance, though I'd gone straight from 20/20 vision to bifocals in my forties. But I really couldn't read any more without them. I sat down on a bench and held my head in my hands. *Help!*

I counted my breaths. In-two-three-four. Out-two-three-four-five. Had I read the big carved sign without them on? When and why had I even taken them off? Was it when I got there, at the other table? I sat for a few more minutes. It was my last chance. If I looked there again and didn't find them, I'd have to give up.

I took a deep breath, got up, and walked to the other table. There, on the ground, were my glasses. How had I not stepped on them?

The answer whooshed through my mind: a thought straight from a childhood steeped in stories of magic, miracles, and superstition. Straight from tales of talking bears, magical lands at the bottom of lakes, and straw woven into gold. Straight from the dim mud-wattle and straw church hall that smelled of whitewash lye and the ghee people rubbed into their hair. Straight from the girl who sat listening, surrounded by people who feared dying from the evil eye. Straight from the Bible stories she read as she half-listened, of Elisha's axe head bobbing to the surface of the river; of Rahab, saved by the red ribbon she hung from her window in the wall of Jericho; of Naaman's leprosy cured in the muddy waters of the Jordan River.

God had protected my glasses. Or was it the fairies?

I clutched them against my heart. I said *Thank you* a thousand times. As adrenalin seeped from my body, I thought of the story of God opening the eyes of the terrified and besieged armies of Israel to see the army of angels on the mountainsides, ready to fight with them.

If all of life is a metaphor, as Trung had said in the Seaside hostel, it must be because our eyes are so easily closed. To the answers of how to heal the wounds of our history; to glasses on the ground. We don't see clearly. We understand so little.

Chapter 15

Walking into the town of Garibaldi, I was still shaken after losing my glasses. I was also worried about the rain, but I was resolutely not thinking about that.

I was early for the next bus around the Tillamook Bay, so I stepped into a bakery across the street from the station. My soul needed reinforcement. Only sugar would do. A maple bar? A glazed donut? A cinnamon roll? Simple decisions often rendered me uncertain, even on a good day. The woman waiting on me snapped that she didn't have all day. I blindly chose. I fumbled my change.

A big group of older men and women had come in for what looked like a club meeting. They all talked at the same time, all shouting. My ears rang. I cowered in a corner.

I was ashamed of annoying the proprietress. I saw myself, as though from the outside, once again the pale blonde girl who looked so ghostly to the people in Maji who'd never seen such a thing. Now I'd morphed into a different ghost, a widow. One with a weird hiking skirt and a gray ponytail. Maybe I'd been alone so much I'd never remember how to manage in society. Maybe I was making myself fit only for a pumpkin shell where I would brood, sing to myself, and eat cold freeze-dried meals.

Panic washed back over me. I'd dropped my glasses. But worse, I hadn't seen them! I could have stepped on them! My cinnamon roll turned to dough in my mouth.

My panic brought back an experience in Portland a few months after Mark died. I got a threatening letter from the DMV, accusing me of driving my car for a year without insurance. I would face a dire fine or imprisonment if I couldn't prove otherwise.

I'd never missed an insurance payment. In my file were the invoices, each one carefully marked with a note, *Paid by check #__*. But years' worth of them were there, unsorted, and my insurance years overlapped two calendar years. I sweated, trying to sort out the dates. I squinted at the numbers, I read and reread, and slipped an invoice into my purse.

In those early months, I couldn't concentrate. My eyes sometimes wouldn't focus. I had lost my partner, but it felt like I'd lost part of my brain. I suddenly needed help from strangers, from people not close in, who didn't love me as much as Mark had. It scared me.

At DMV, the woman in front of me had a problem that took at least forty-five minutes. I finally stepped up to the window and gave my certificate of good payment behavior to the gentleman there. When he pushed it back to me, pointing to the wrong date, I burst into tears.

He had a kind smile. He may have patted my hand. "Just run home. The right one must be there and you'll be back here and done in no time."

His kindness made it worse. I felt even more vulnerable—what if he had been mean to me? I drove home crying so hard I could hardly see. I shouted out loud at myself. "Pay attention! Why can't you pay attention?" I pounded on the steering wheel. "How are you going to manage if you can't pay attention?"

I had survived those early months of turmoil, tempest, and disruption. I had thought I could pay attention again. I had thought I could keep myself safe. But I had almost stepped on my glasses.

I quickly finished my coffee and moved to the bench outside the tiny terminal in Garibaldi. My breath, pulse, and mind returned to what felt like sanity.

The bus dropped me in Tillamook. From there, I would take a back road to Oceanside, where I had a room reserved at Three Arch Inn. Check-in at the hotel wasn't until mid-afternoon. I had time to explore. I'd gotten used to what struck me so oddly at first, that I would only hike for a few hours every day. My feet, not daylight hours, were the limiting factor.

I walked around downtown, looking for coffee, dawdling in front of display windows for boutiques I wouldn't go into in my pack and hiking skirt.

A sandwich sign pointed me to the 2nd Street Coffee Shop. The door was open. *Prairie Home Companion* blasted out to passersby, of whom I was the only one at the moment. I stepped into a tiny space so crammed with junk that I gasped, as though I might run short of oxygen. One small bistro table was clear. Every other usable wall and floor space was covered with shelves, every shelf was crammed with China dolls, old metal dump trucks, cloth-covered books so old their titles had worn off the spines, a blow-up Mickey Mouse, a giant fleece carrot, hand-blown glass floats speckled with bubbles.

"Hello?" I called.

Garrison Keeler ignored me. I leaned my pack against the little table uncertainly. A bumper sticker on the front of the old wooden counter announced, *I've been Shanghaied!* The laminated top was plastered with cartoons. I stepped over to read them and saw, off to the right, a two-foot-wide door with an old metal *Restroom* sign. I squeezed in, barely able to turn around, planning my apology to the owner, who would surely be back when I emerged. But he wasn't.

I stepped back out onto the sidewalk. A young woman came out of the back of a kitchen next door. Following her came a blast of steam that smelled of beef grease and hot oil.

"Do you know where the proprietor of the coffee shop might be?" I asked.

"No clue. He steps out sometimes."

Back in the café, since I was alone, I sat down and unpacked my lunch. A couple came in and looked around. I had taken down a copy of *The Next Whole Earth Catalog* that was so worn the pages were soft and rounded at the corners. I pretended to read until it was obvious that they were wondering why I didn't hop to.

"I'm waiting, also," I said. I pointed to the *Shanghaied* bumper sticker. "Maybe he left that message for us."

They chuckled, then stood awkwardly for a few more minutes, their whispered conversation drowned by a song by some live band in St. Paul, Minnesota. Then they left. I ate my lunch and apologized to half a dozen more would be customers. *Prairie Home Companion was ending.*

Finely the proprietor returned, a geezer in the Oregon country uniform of jeans and flannel, and stepped behind the counter without a word about where he'd been. "I've had this place since 2001," he said, making my long-awaited latte. "Too long. Nobody wants it."

When I finished my drink, I tucked away my journal. But I still couldn't always pay attention. I walked away and left my wide-brimmed hat hanging from the bistro chair. By the time I missed it, it had certainly been absorbed into the clutter of the 2nd Street Coffee Shop.

I walked to the long bridge over the Tillamook River, just beyond a tributary, the Trask River. I hadn't known there was a river named for that *most restless Dam fool Trask*. If the book was right, Trask and the Tillamooks did the best they could for each other in that train wreck of American settlement.

I walked as fast as I could across the bridge, so narrow that it had no shoulder at all. Farms spread out on either side of the country road leading to the east side of Cape Mears. After the trials of the highway and town, I took a deep breath of air that had brushed across water and smiled.

Chapter 16

The roadway next to the bay once again narrowed, hugging blasted stone on the left and dropping off to rocky seawalls on the right. Jagged, half-rotted posts stuck out of the lapping water, as though there had once been a giant pier. The ditch under the cliff was packed with reed canary grass, the invasive whose dense roots smother native cattails and other marshy plants. I hoped the brushy willows I'd planted in my seasonal stream in Salem were doing their job of fighting the reed canary grass invasion, and now I turned my face away, seeing it in the ditch.

I was walking north, on the bay side of the Cape Mears Loop, before it rounded and swung south to the town of Oceanside. At the top of the cape, I came to a sign that looked more like a newspaper article than a historic marker. I hadn't heard of Bayocean Park before, one more town memorializing the nature it had paved over. Are there any two random nature nouns that, mashed together, *don't* sound like a housing development? Meadow Springs. Pine Lake. Hill Stream. Bay Ocean.

Bayocean Park was a resort town, built on the sand spit that protects Tillamook Bay from the tide. Developers in 1910 built stores, a bakery, a swimming pool, a dance pavilion, two hotels and—its pride and joy—a giant *natatorium*, with a 160-foot pool of warmed seawater and artificial waves, built right in front of the dune at the foot of the real sea. They promoted the town as the Atlantic City of the West.

Warmed seawater was actually a brilliant idea, as anyone knows who's stuck a toe in the frigid Pacific. Wealthy guests from Portland came to Bayocean Park, first by private yacht, then by railroad.

Later, in the museum in Tillamook, I saw dozens of black and white photos of revelers enjoying "nature" in the natatorium.

Problems came to Bayocean Park when the communities of Tillamook County went to the Corps of Engineers for a jetty to improve shipping. Engineers worried that building only one jetty would change wave patterns, but the communities insisted, and they were funding it. Shifting tides began eroding the Bayocean spit immediately. By the 1940s, the sea was eating fifty feet per year into the beach and washing into the town during storms. In 1952, a November storm opened a mile-wide breach in the spit. The ocean also roared into Tillamook Bay, flooding oyster farms and threatening the town and even inland farms.

The same citizens who insisted on one jetty quickly funded a second. We inhabit our own bodies so fully, it's hard to be content to be what we are—mere weekend guests on earth. The sea went back to work, in its oceanic mystery, building up the sand on the spit.

In 2011, the renewed spit caught the eye of a modern Portland developer. He submitted plans for an eco-resort featuring luxury tents, horse-riding, kayaking, a marina, aqua-tourism, and a lab station for marine research. But his application was sketchy on details about transportation, sanitation, and potable water. And the spit lies unprotected from a tsunami, lying far from rescue stations, with no higher ground for evacuation. This time, wisdom prevailed and the proposal was rejected. Out where there was once a dance pavilion and a natatorium, nature has again found its wild and fragile balance.

And tsunamis are a real threat, with the long Cascadia Subduction Zone about a hundred miles off the West Coast. I have a friend whose geologist husband won't allow anyone in his family to overnight in the sea level towns of the Oregon coast.

I had been looking with some concern at the tsunami escape maps in the campgrounds and sea-level towns I passed through. *If there's an earthquake, shelter until the trembling stills....A tsunami can follow within minutes....Don't wait for the warning whistle.*

I'd studied the escape routes. But in a strange town, what were my chances of remembering the right streets? The anxiety my friend's husband feels had seeped in. I'd started looking around for my own escape routes as I walked, as I camped. I would drop my pack (or stumble out of my tent) and run for high ground, wherever I could see it. *Was this or that bluff high enough? Would I be able to run fast enough at my age? In my hiking boots?* I was more than willing to participate in our corporate delusion that there must be a way to outrun death when it comes for us.

Both the 1964 Alaska earthquake and a 2011 earthquake offshore from Japan sent tsunamis to Oregon. The waves that climbed 220 feet high in Alaska were still 13 feet high here. In Japan, waves rose 130 feet high and swept away tens of thousands of people. Ten hours later, the ocean sloshed six and a half feet high on the Oregon coast and killed four people.

But those aren't the scary ones. Earthquakes far away give our coastal cities time to set off their modern warning sirens. I would have hours to get off the beach.

The urgency only comes if land shifts under water off our shore. Geologists say that forty times through the millennia, the Cascadia subduction zone has suddenly come unstuck and shifted somewhere along the miles from Vancouver BC to northern California. These shifts have caused massive quakes. They are called *megathrust events*.

Coastal First Nations (in Canada) and Native American peoples (in the US) tell stories of the last one, an earthquake followed by a tsunami that swept away entire villages. Some groups even have a count of the generations since it happened.

For too long, scientists were dismissive of that oral history. But the Japanese live with frequent earthquakes and have been keeping written records since the fifth century. In January 1700, the Japanese recorded a mystery—an orphan tsunami with no warning earthquake anywhere on the eastern Pacific Rim. As research developed and the globe shrank, other data began linking that tsunami with an earthquake in Oregon.

The Native American stories say the earthquake struck at night in the winter, just after people went to bed.

Eventually the scientists in their lab coats realized the puzzle pieces fit. It takes ten hours for waves from the US West Coast to ripple over to Japan. That means the Cascadia plates popped loose at 9:00 PM on January 26, 1700. The Japanese tsunami went on for eighteen hours. By calculating the volume of water displacement, geologists know Oregon experienced an 8.7-9.2 magnitude earthquake.

Brian Atwater, a Washington state geologist, says, "If you were to let a hurricane like Isabel (in 2003) run for 70 days, the energy released in the winds would be equivalent to a magnitude 9 earthquake."

Now the geologists have also found *ghost forests* off our coast. Sitka spruce stumps in the ocean show thick growth rings through 1699 and then—sudden inundation and death by salt water.

Pretty cool what they can figure out. Unless you're walking the coast and wondering how many minutes you'd have and how high you'd have to climb. Some native groups are moving their coastal communities to higher ground as the geological studies warn us more and more clearly of what will come. That seems so smart but utterly impossible for the rest of us.

I've chosen to live in Portland. The chance of our city being toast ever niggles in the dark depths of Portlanders' minds. A vague threat like the threat of getting cancer—what can we do about it? I moved to Portland before all this research came together. Should I move out now? What are my chances of convincing my siblings and all my friends to move with me? Should the government force our hands, shutting down the city of Portland and helping us rebuild inland before the Big One forces us? If we were purely rational beings, cities like Portland and New Orleans might be packed up without a second thought. Our physical bodies want the comfort we find in the physically familiar—relocation for any reason feels like pain and trauma.

So the threat of a disaster that could happen but hasn't, one that would be truly traumatic, feels unlikely and we stay. We say *hopefully not in my lifetime,* and go on loving our tree and flower-festooned city. Mt. Hood watches over us in calm and beauty, whatever future days may bring. We drive off on weekends to Cascade Mountain lakes in one direction and the ocean in the other. We tuck our survival kits—some water, some canned food, and a flashlight—in a corner of our sheds or basements. We cross our fingers.

And I, whenever I leave Portland for the weekend, idly wonder whether the Big One will hit while I'm gone. Why don't I wake up in the morning every day, and wonder whether the Big One will hit while I'm there? It's a strange trick of my mind, to be so settled with the risk I'm taking.

Here's my retelling of an ancient Mesopotamian tale: a man from Baghdad came suddenly face to face with Death in the marketplace in Jerusalem. Death looked startled.

The man immediately hired the fastest horse in Jerusalem and galloped for home, hundreds of miles away. When one mount tired, he hired another. He rode day and night, outrunning death. He arrived in Baghdad as dawn broke on Saturday morning. He stumbled into his home, exhausted.

Death was waiting for him there, smiling. "Welcome. I couldn't imagine how you would make it to our appointment in time!"

On the cape road, after I passed the sign with the history and photos of Bayocean Park, I rounded the top of the peninsula and passed the trail to the Cape Mears Lighthouse. It's the smallest Oregon lighthouse, and much tamer than Terrible Tilly. Only thirty-eight feet tall, it sits on the side of the cliff, two hundred and seventeen feet above sea level. It can be seen a full twenty-one miles out to sea.

Rare peregrine falcon pairs have been nesting on the cliff since 1987. Park rangers have built a viewpoint so tourists can see, in the wild, earth's fastest creature.

It was ironic. By traveling on foot, observing my surroundings in slowly passing detail, I couldn't explore. I didn't have it in me to walk the spur out to the lighthouse and back. And so, I passed by the signs for it and the octopus-tree, a giant Sitka spruce with no central trunk, whose tentacles grow upward. I'd have to come back someday in a car.

The road swung away from the cliff, with its windblown brush, into the Cape Mears National Wildlife Refuge, established in the 1930s to protect some of the last old-growth forest of Oregon. And then, ahead of me, cement posts and aluminum cattle fencing barred the road: *No access*. A huge sinkhole gaped in the right lane. Beyond the sink hole, the road buckled and split.

I stood there for a long time. I dug out the OCT map. Back in Tillamook, I could find a hotel, of course. I could add a day to my chart. But it would be twice as far to go back to Tillamook as to go on.

I studied the sinkhole.

I would never have driven a car on the narrow, intact, left lane. But little old me, with my little old pack; the sinkhole would hardly know we were there. Another far-away, unlikely risk—a sinkhole spontaneously caving and swallowing me whole—seemed like the stuff of those fairy tales. I slipped by and walked deeper into the forest, enchanted to think that now I was the only human being on that entire half of the peninsula.

Chapter 17

The western side of the Cape Mears headland is almost untouched. Some of the spruce and hemlocks are over 200 feet tall and hundreds of years old. The silence, as I walked along the buckled road, enveloped me. It was a breathing silence. There was not a whisper of breeze, so far below the green overstory. Not a splash of sunlight. On the ground, moss, ferns, and samples of all the native plants I'd added on my farm in Salem covered the soil: serviceberry, ocean spray, goat's beard, Douglas spirea. Bird call was a mere murmur. The light looked green. The air smelled green. My tiny wisps of carbon dioxide were instantly absorbed. In exchange, oxygen poured over me like a waterfall.

If I always understood, like I did in that moment, that in my essence I belonged in this world just as every tree there, would I worry about being alone? I walked on among the giant trees, humbled.

I was aching by the time I got to Oceanside. A sign on Three Arch Inn's lobby door said *Back Soon!* I sat on the cement steps, rested my elbows on my knees and my chin on my hand, waiting, looking out at the three arch-shaped rocks. They stand up to waves that have been beating against them for millennia. They are what's left of a flood of lava. The rock all around each of them has cracked and fallen, piece by piece, into the ocean. Maybe the sand below on the beach was once part of them. How could so much rock be gone, conquered just by water? How long could they stand, three punctuation marks of stone out in the ocean?

It had been a calming day. My emotions had been washing against me but I too wouldn't topple.

A tattooed young hostess named Ahnjayla, with braids and lots of earrings, got back from her errands and checked me in. I shyly shared my reason for being there. The room she walked me to, on the second floor, looked out over the ocean through the biggest picture window I'd ever seen. On the walls, photos of rocks, tide pools and bright blue, orange, and yellow starfish shone down through unstreaked glass.

Ahnjayla assured me that the starfish are real. They're sea stars, she said. They stay behind in the tide pools when the ocean retreats. To see them, I needed to slip through a tunnel. She pointed out the window. From above, the headland looked like the paws of a huge stone beast who lay on the coast with its toes in the ocean. One of its toes was pierced.

I asked about a bus schedule, and Ahnjayla came back up a few minutes later to where I was now standing in the hallway reading brochures. Even the hallways and stairwells at the Three Arch Inn were wood-lined and light—white oak, maybe, or native alder.

She handed me the papers. "I have a gift for you."

"Oh, thank you," I said, and opened the tide schedule to September.

"Not that. Can we step into your room?" She followed me in, leaving the door open. "I don't want other guests to hear."

I set the papers on the foot of the bed.

"We're so small here in Oceanside, we only have one bus a day, and it's..." She sounded apologetic. "It's at 6:49 tomorrow morning. You only just got here. And now it's high tide. You can't get through to see the sea stars."

I was watching her face. I didn't understand that the disappointment in her voice was on my behalf.

"So, we want to give you an extra day here. You have to see them!"

"I really can't afford..."

"Comped, I mean. I want to do this for you." She stood between me and the open door of my room, all that light from the window on her face. "When you told me about your husband, and what you're doing, it gave me goosebumps. I've got Native blood. I'm very intuitive. You're amazing."

Maybe all that oxygen among the trees had put me in a daze. I was astounded, but astounded in slow motion. I thanked her and there was no awkwardness between us. We stood in the room, in the light, and she talked. She told me that she was epileptic, that the last time she fell, she broke her back and fractured her skull. She told me about the metal staples that hold her head together; about the epilepsy medication that costs four hundred dollars a month. "So I'm a pothead instead." She threw back her head and laughed.

She said working at the inn was the best job she'd ever had. She'd worked in a group home in Tucson before Oregon. "Here, it's like being on vacation every afternoon. And the morning is just, like—one more bed to make."

I loved her. I wanted my life to be calm like hers.

She told me the desserts at the café across the street, Rosanne's Cafe, were as good as they sounded, and I could get supper there, too. She said people regularly eat their desserts first at Rosanne's. I laughed at that, and doubted that I'd be able to make it a habit. Nobody changes that much, do they?

When Ahnjayla left, I pulled an armchair closer to the window and put my feet up on the glass coffee table. Out on the hypnotic swells, whitecaps popped up here and there. The sun wove its way through strips of stratus clouds on its way down toward the horizon. Shadows zipped across the sand.

I'd become a cup. A cup that could hold what other people poured into it. I was trying to hold my own story, make room for its surprise ending, and I'd become big enough to hold other stories as well. My taxi driver's addicted boyfriend. John's accident. Ahnjayla's suffering and injuries and joy. And instead of burdening me further, my cup holding their stories of suffering lightened mine.

I looked at my pack leaning against the wall, and saw that somewhere along the way, the pink and turquoise beads had broken off. They must be nestled in all their unnatural colors among the woody fibers on the trail. Did it matter that my talisman had become litter? I laid my head back and closed my eyes.

Later, in the afternoon sunshine, I hauled my pack out of the hotel room and down to a grassy knoll overlooking the ocean. I laid out the damp tent, the wet rainfly, and the half-wet sleeping bag. I looked around for anyone who would take offense, but no one was paying attention. I sat on the grass nearby to write in my journal.

Among the few papers I'd folded and slipped into the soft notebook were notes from a CD—lectures by David Whyte, a philosopher and poet. The paper on either side of the fold was no longer white but beige, from my camp-dirty fingers. I had lain in my tent every evening, reading a few lines by my headlamp, underlining any sentence or phrase that spoke to me. By now, almost everything was underlined. I had started double-underlining. If only his words would settle from my mind to my heart. To my gut. Even with all the re-reading and underlining, day after day my emotions washed me out to sea and I had to paddle in again, against the tide, to shore and solid ground.

I'd discovered David Whyte on another journey, from my tiny house in Portland to the town of Bend to see Jesse and Beth, driving for the first time that far alone. Cathy had given me a stack of music CDs and suggested I get an audiobook. I stopped by the library in a hurry and dashed through the stacks to find the audiobook section. It stretched from floor to ceiling. How on earth would I find something that would interest me for three hours on the road? My eyes, in all that clutter, homed right in on it—*What to Remember When Walking.*

I listened to NPR news on the way out of town. I listened one time through Joan Baez's melancholy songs on Cathy's CD. Then, with a sense of anticipation, I fumbled the first audio book CD out of its sleeve and slipped it in. I had never heard of David Whyte. He began with his own translation of Dante, lost in a dark forest.

I listened on, enchanted.

I had wondered often whether my life had always been so buffeted by the unexpected—both by difficulties I'd never imagined and by synchronicities—or whether somehow Mark's death had delivered me over a gap and into an entirely different world. As though I had stepped from solid land into a sailboat on the ocean, subject to all the winds and calms, the sun and the thunder, the unseen and unseeable currents of a wild and uncontrolled world.

Finding David Whyte's CD was an unforeseen moment. I'd been given something I hadn't asked for. But the more I listened to it, the more I wondered. When was David Whyte going to talk about walking? Lots to remember, yes, but what about the walking? Finally, I flipped the CD case shut and took my eyes off the road long enough to reread the cover: *What to Remember When Waking.*

What to remember when you wake up in a dark wood. That's what David Whyte was lecturing on. I was a cynic when it came to philosophy. I was intimidated by poetry. It was only my rushed skimming that had opened David Whyte's thoughtfulness to me. If I had read the title correctly, I would have sneered at the notion of waking up to life, becoming more enlightened, blah blah blah.

Driving the highway to Bend, with Douglas firs whipping by the window in the Mount Hood National Forest, I laughed out loud at the trick that had been played on me—that's what it felt like. I couldn't stop. I giggled for several miles as I climbed over the shoulder of Mount Hood on my way across the Cascades Mountain range to the high desert of Central Oregon. *Waking* to a new life, *walking* to a new life, they were the same. Mr. Whyte and Mr. Bridges, of the *Transitions* book, were my new my gurus.

On the hillside outside the Three Arch Hotel, after a half hour of rereading David Whyte, I checked on my damp tent and sleeping bag. They had dried in the sun and ocean breeze. I left them where they lay and went back to my spot on the grass.

As it turned out, I was in Oceanside in the exact middle of my walk. The walking had been steeper, longer, more painful than I'd expected, but both the forests and the beaches had been more beautiful. Now I'd run into rain. And now I knew what I'd suspected—that my tent was not waterproof. But Mom always used to say, *A little rain won't hurt you.* And one shower at dawn the day before didn't mean the rain was starting in earnest. I would rest in Ahnjayla's hospitality, eat pie, and then go back to whatever surprises would be delivered to me on the trail.

Chapter 18

On the hill in Oceanside, I watched over the tent as it billowed in the breeze and thought of how I'd waited for Mark's death, weeping and asking out loud on my walks along the irrigation canal in Bend, *What will become of me?* How tough was it going to be to fully inhabit, to even embrace, my new life alone?

I'd conceived this pilgrimage for closure, for testing—*how strong am I?* And then it had taken on a life of its own: planning, preparing, launching. It had become a project, something the book on happiness said happy people have.

And while Mark was sick, walking—the simple act of placing one foot and then the other—had been a healing routine I needed every day. Walking bound mind and body together, like the whip-stitch I'd learned as a ten-year-old about to go to boarding school, needing to re-hem half a dozen full skirts. Hemming had been a hypnosis to soothe my anxieties as a girl. Walking was soothing me now as a woman. I would walk on pilgrimage and wake to my new life alone.

I found—many people find—that even by myself in the forest I didn't feel alone. I had nothing to do but walk in the presence of trees, and it was enough. I was never alone on the beach, with the tide and the busy sea birds. Out on the trail, I was either numb with fatigue or I was St. Francis: *Brother sun, sister moon.*

It was being alone in a house, in a neighborhood, making decisions alone for the rest of my life that frightened me. David Whyte talked about the courage it takes to interact honestly with our circumstances. He asked why we quibble about the details of daily life when our minds could be full of delight. We are unique and marvelous creatures in a marvelous world. But without Mark to help me think, I had half a brain. Without him beside me, I had only half a body.

Even up on the knoll in Oceanside, the breeze smelled of seaweed. Clouds gathered and lowered over the surf, turning the ocean deep green. A few drops spat. I jumped up and rolled the tent, rain fly, and sleeping bag into a bundle and stuffed them into my pack. I would move my contemplations back to the easy chair, the coffee table, and the huge picture window.

That was my intention. But when I got inside, the desire to contemplate had also gone behind a cloud. I stretched out on the bed for my first nap in weeks. I woke, groggy and depressed. Drops were ticking against the window, and the horizon was muffled in fog.

I heated water in the hotel's electric kettle to reconstitute my freeze-dried Pad Thai. As I ate, I imagined the ounces of noodles and sauce I would not have to carry any further. That's what I was doing, metabolizing what I could and going on, lighter.

That the food was warm lifted my mood a little. My years in Ethiopia, in South Sudan, had left me vulnerable to reproachful voices: *How can you be depressed when you have so much more? How can you be having a hard time when your life is so much easier?* I would go on lighter if I could walk away from existential guilt, embrace my gifts with gratitude. How does a person do that? I slipped into the second-hand merino wool hoodie, and ran between raindrops to Roseanne's Cafe for dessert.

I nibbled at a lemon sponge pudding drizzled with sauce made from Oregon's own Marionberries. Mark would have been vibrating with pleasure, sitting across from me with a serving of such richness. I swallowed hard, looking out over the gray sea.

I was supposed to be walking away from lots of things, most urgently from mourning for the loss of my husband, my marriage, my farm. Walking it off and going on, content to be a city girl now. Grief is so deeply selfish. I couldn't bear that my life would never be as it had been. Lemon pudding burned in my cheeks.

Our marriage had been like swing dancing, spinning away from each other and back. My closeness was so essential to Mark, it frightened and silenced him. His loyalty to me was so deep, it threatened to smother. We had both needed space from the pressure.

My kids had known me, for the last twenty years, as the mom who traveled alone for work. They had expected me to bounce with verve into the new adventure of my singleness.

We had missed how it was Mark tethering me that let me do so much alone. Now I was lonelier than we expected. It shocked them—and me—how unbalanced I felt after he died. Hadn't I always craved space? Now I had too much.

I shouldn't have been so surprised. In sixty-four years, I had never lived alone. I went from a chaotic family of eight to mission boarding schools—rooms just big enough for four girls in bunk beds to share two dressers and an iron rod for hanging up the dresses we were required to wear to class.

All my life, I'd been surrounded by people. Not always people I felt close to, but always others I bumped up against, who elbowed back at me with their own needs and desires. They had held me balanced on this precarious earth like trees in the forest. Now I was like a city tree that might fall in a winter storm because there's nothing to break the wind.

I finished my dessert and walked back over to the Three Arch Inn. I filled the tub and added the scented bath salts I had bought in Tillamook, promising myself a restorative soak. When we were young and thin, Mark and I had slipped into hot baths together before the days of hot tubs. His legs hairy, mine shaved smooth. His skin pink, mine with a slightly warmer cast. He always got out first so I could slide down under the surface and wash my long, straight, hippie hair.

Cradled in hot water alone in Three Arch Inn, I saw that I had thought if I made a pilgrimage, a spiritual pilgrimage, with contemplation and prayer and a journal—if I did it right—everything would work out on the other side. Now I saw that *working out* had meant magic. Like the biblical Job, everything would be restored to me double. No matter how difficult marriage had sometimes felt, how much I wanted it back.

Instead, David Whyte was talking about pain and difficulty inevitably cycling through our lives. I didn't want life to be like that. And William Bridges had his own bad news about transitions, that they go on longer than we think we can bear. What if the happiness book was right, and I never adapted to widowhood?

Back in the evening chill of the room, with wet hair down my back, I snuggled into the armchair and tucked my feet under me. A line of light the color of banked embers had broken through the clouds just above the horizon. I watched it fade, grateful to be inside on a night that threatened to go on wet and cold for hours.

I woke the next day and stretched out on the wide bed. Against my arms and legs, the sheets felt silky smooth. The spacious mattress didn't rustle. I had a full day to rest. What a wonderful gift.

As I turned on my fully-charged phone, I realized it was Kenny's birthday. I texted him my love. Kenny's birthday always signaled the downhill side of September, with sunsets now crowding afternoons that had been so long for so brief a time.

I left my bag of granola on the counter and went downstairs—breakfast is a meal hard to spoil. I stepped into the Brewin' in the Wind Café on the ground floor of the inn and was blasted by Chicago's brass on the radio—*Does Anybody Really Know What Time It Is?* With the music came the twenty-year-old I once was, and the feelings of those years: so confused, so disillusioned, so frustrated. Maybe I had never changed at all.

Peace signs littered the café wall around the iconic silkscreen poster from the '70s, with its childlike drawing of a daisy: *War is not healthy for children and other living creatures.* Buddhist prayer flags spelled PEACE. Dr. Martin Luther King Jr.'s photo on another poster: *We have to live together as brothers and sisters or perish together as fools.* Mark would have laughed and nudged me with his elbow: *Your kind of place!* The waitress delivered ice water as Steely Dan picked up the pace, twanging his guitar riffs, *Go Back Jack, Do It Again.*

I'd been young and beautiful when Mark and I met up as almost-adults in Washington DC during cherry blossom season. He rowed me on the Potomac. We picnicked on the Mall, and I met him there again for a concert, Prokle Harem, for pity's sake, and we lounged in the dark on a blanket on the grass and shared a glowing, sweet-smelling joint of the other kind of grass.

I felt a surge of gratitude for all that had flowed from that time in DC: my kids and all the memories, even the difficult ones. They had brought me to this life in this café in this town. For a moment I could feel its richness. I ordered a veggie omelet and opened my journal.

The fire alarm shrieked. My pen scratched a jagged mark on the page. A guy in jeans and a dirty t-shirt ran in. The waitress dashed by. I covered my ears and watched, alert for a signal to evacuate—a grease fire in the kitchen? Flames climbing up the wall?

The alarm went blessedly silent. The waitress reappeared, a little breathless, and smiled at me. I went back to my journal.

Four Strong Winds. My sister Janie and I had played it on the guitar we shared in college. We sang it in the dry, dusty backyard of an ancient farmhouse in Eastern Oregon, sitting in a porch swing with old plastic pillow covers. It was the year of my grandparents' fiftieth wedding anniversary and a reunion with my twenty-five cousins. Winds blowing lonely. What a lovely phrase. Maybe I'd always been prone to melancholy.

The alarm went off again. "The guy's working on it," the waitress shouted.

As she cleared my plate, it shrilled for the third time, drowning out Cat Stevens as he crooned his warning. I wasn't anyone's Baby any more, but I still needed more than a smile to get by.

I'd been smart, after all, to choose a hard walk, not the cocoon of a retreat center. Smart to bump my feelings of sadness and fear against the need to do the next practical thing. In my journal, I wrote about the Buddhist prayer flags untouched by the fire alarm that kept shrieking. Peace could be found even in the Blowin' in the Wind Café on a melancholy morning.

Chapter 19

I read in my room that morning in Oceanside, glancing up from *Trask* to the ocean that clawed its way relentlessly up the beach and then fell back, its reach a little shorter each time. I finished the book. I wrote in my journal.

When I got restless, I walked a few miles south to the tiny town of Netarts and back. People come to Oceanside to play on the beach, to slip through and see the sea stars, to take pictures of the three arches. It was clear that people go to Netarts to fish.

The tiny town with its own tiny bay smelled like fish. Boats bobbed in quiet water that lapped against the sand. Groups of children ran and shouted. I walked as far as Happy Camp Road, peeking into the cabins: plastic tablecloths, beach towels draped over couches, shoes of various sizes scattered around the doors. For a moment, as in the forest, I felt not like an observer, but like a co-participant in the life of Netarts. I turned at the end of town and got back to Oceanside at low tide.

The tunnel through the headland was open, beginning as a rough cement vault with small square holes for light. When the cement petered out a few feet in, the tunnel became a pebble and sand-strewn tube of rough stone about 100 feet long. The rounded ceiling over my head made me want to stoop. I had been walking over ancient lava. Now I was encased in it—stone that began as liquid somewhere in Idaho.

What looked like a petrified log five or six feet long lay on the ground halfway through. In the dim light, I stood and stared. It must have been a tree that was toppled and carried by lava all that way. Dropped from the ceiling to the floor when they blasted the tunnel.

Wait. I was imagining things in the shadowed light. How could a tree survive the heat and not burn to ash? It must be a driftwood log, floated into the tunnel by a king tide, transformed by the dim light into something ancient. How easy it is to see the wrong thing.

As I stepped out of the tunnel, I saw that the headland itself bifurcates, each side a bluff that extends into the sea, cradling Tunnel Beach between them. It was a minus-level low tide that day. In the pools left behind, I found the sea stars. They draped and oozed over each other and over the rough black rocks, spilling down the sides in all their startling colors: burgundy, blue, orange. They were not only colorful, but fatter than the classic washed-out-terracotta colored starfish. They made me think of peanut butter poured out oily, then solidified into dryish blobs down the side of a bowl. I drifted from one lava stone pool to another. Anemones in pastel shades of green and turquoise breathed water in the bottoms and waved semi-transparent tentacles in hopes of enticing prey.

Back at the hotel, my room felt stale. I had a long afternoon and evening ahead. No book. I sat with my journal and found I had nothing to say.

Was it the break from walking so hard that was making me sad in Oceanside? I really thought I'd be done with this. How long would it go on, the dreary preview my mind created for the movie of my new life? The hours and hours alone that I would have to figure out some way to fill? We had both always thought Mark would die first. But I thought by then I'd be *old*. A widow! I couldn't get the word out of my mind.

I got up for Kleenex and wrote in my journal that I had been living like a sailboat with its sail let out, catching the wind and racing across the water, trying to outrun my fear and get to the other side.

Mark had shown me the magic of running before the wind when we were first married and he took me out in his father's tiny sailboat. There's no resistance moving with the speed of the wind. It's eerie. Utterly silent, no matter how hard the wind is blowing. There's no other way to be in wind and not hear it. When you don't yield to the wind, that's when it roars in your ears.

Out on the water, a sailor usually has to do the hard noisy work of tacking, using the power of the wind but controlling where it takes them. I wrote, *I just want to let the sails out and run. I have children. I have grandchildren, but I feel so lost.* A woman of my age should be braver; should be stronger. I was afraid, not only of my new life alone, but of all these feelings and thoughts.

I stopped writing and sketched the arch furthest out in the ocean. There are three big stacks and six little ones. When I got home, I looked them up. The websites are vague about which rock is which: Storm, Seal, Shag, Finley.

At the turn of the 19th century, Mr. Finley had seen what other people didn't, that the seeming vastness of nature was finite. He and a friend rowed out to the arches in a dory. They took provisions for two weeks and set up camp on the rocks, which were slippery with guano. After their first night, suffering through the shrill calls of the birds and the booming surf, Finley wrote, *It felt like we had spent the night on the top of a jagged picket fence.*

But they stayed the full two weeks and took photographs, which they carried to Washington DC and showed President Roosevelt in person. They begged him to put a stop to tugboat trips out with weekend tourists to slaughter the sea lions, with sportsmen who used tufted puffins for target practice, with locals who collected seabird eggs to sell in the coastal communities because there were so few chickens.

Roosevelt declared the rocks Three Arches National Refuge, one of the earliest protected wildlife sites in the US. It was the first one west of the Mississippi and is still the smallest. Both tufted puffins and the common murre or awk—a bird that can fly but stands upright like a sharp-beaked penguin—breed there. And Seal Rock is the only pupping site for the larger of Oregon's two sea lion species.

When I woke on my second morning in the Three Arch Inn, I crawled into the armchair to meditate. A spiritual advisor had given me a book called *Centering Prayer and Inner Awakening* five years earlier.

Mark and I had listened to a CD set by Abbot Thomas Keating. I started meditating for twenty minutes every morning, focusing on internal quiet, not on a subject, a word, or an object. Thomas Merton recommends silence as a way of *finding one's deepest center, awakening the profound depths of our being.* It helped tame my emotional chaos after Dad died.

Mark tried, but he said sitting silently just upset him. He had too many thoughts. He didn't like seeing how cluttered his mind was. I stuck with it. Morning after morning, I stumbled from bed into my office, to an armchair, a bright blue fleece throw, and an orange plastic timer.

To begin my meditation practice, I had learned to pray Bishop Keating's three releasing prayers: *I release the need for power and control. I release the need for safety and security. I release the need for love and esteem.* Father Keating said when we try to meet these three needs with people or things, they pull us away from God.

Then I sat quietly every day. I used a sacred word that I carefully chose. The word signaled to my mind that I would return to stillness whenever my thoughts started to rev up. I also did as Abbot Keating suggested, and imagined myself at the bottom of a river, with thoughts as boats floating downstream above me. Their anchors hung down and I let them float on by. Experiencing quiet every morning had begun to calm me.

Now, in Oceanside, I prayed my releasing prayers and settled in to return to quiet as often as I needed. I had been meditating for long enough by then, I didn't need a timer any more. I could sense when twenty minutes had passed.

I opened my eyes. Out the window, the westernmost rock glowed golden. I gasped. Only that one shapely arch, a sea stack of enduring basalt, had caught the morning sun. The ocean gave it a lacy collar and rippled around it in silver and pewter. The other rocks stood guard in dull gray. I watched until the gold faded and the sun fully lighted the sky. I felt as though I'd been given a promise: beauty would endure, even when I was only enduring. Test and see. This is enough.

Downstairs, they'd gotten the fire alarm fixed. Jim Croce sang about time in a bottle. I turned wistful. If it was 1970 again and I was young and had the chance, would I really want to change anything? All my sadness and worry was dimly marbled with curiosity. Mark's deep introversion had bounded me into a very quiet life. Maybe in the future I would have more friends, have more fun, have new hobbies and interests. If I could just get over the emptiness I had fallen into.

Back in my room with the huge picture window, I studied Bonnie Henderson's description of the next section of the OCT. It was a mess. After that splendid time in the wildlife refuge between Tillamook and Oceanside, the walk was about to peter out again.

To get beyond Netarts Bay, where the beach is replaced by a three-foot rock wall between saltwater and road, Bonnie advised catching a ride from that mythical boatman and walking the spit to the hiker biker camp at Cape Lookout State Park. I wasn't going to fall for that one again.

And from Oceanside south, Cape Lookout and Cape Kiwanda are so rough with lava that Highway 101 swings inland, away from the beach. I needed to revert to the Kurtz Walk 'n Ride version of the OCT for a couple of days.

As I checked out of the hotel, Ahnjayla fussed at me about the rain. "You had such a powerful effect on me," she said again. I was mystified. Maybe it was because we were both living intensely, our sense of fleeting life so close in.

I admitted to her that my tent wasn't waterproof, but I made light of it, embarrassed by her solicitude.

I waited on the bench across the street until the bus pulled in, then chucked my pack into the luggage hold and claimed a front seat. The driver jammed into gear. Suddenly, Ahnjayla dashed across the street and banged on the door. It opened again with a whoosh.

She stepped up and stuffed something blue, something that crackled in its cellophane wrapper, onto my lap. "Take this!" She waved to the driver and hopped back off.

I threw kisses as the bus pulled out.

Her gift was a tarp. Amazing—Ahnjayla happened to have a tarp, still in its wrapper, just the size of my tent. And she thought of me. Through the cellophane, I fingered the rivets.

The bus stopped for others—the hidden people without cars on the coast, those who depend on others to go where they want to go. Riders hobbled on with canes. Some wore jeans and t-shirts, some wore dingy polyester pants and stretched out sweaters. Most seemed fragile financially, mentally, or emotionally.

The driver knew many of them by name. He was warm and tender. Riders asked him with concern about those they hadn't seen in a while. Then, as the passengers chatted, the driver and I had a literary conversation about *Trask*. This was the deeper truth: none of us were alone.

Chapter 20

Fortified by kindness, humbled by how permeable the walls between strangers can be, I got off the bus at the entrance of Cape Lookout State Park. The miles-long driveway to the campground meandered, lush with coastal trees and ferns. As I stood at the entrance, trying to figure out where to camp, I could hear the ocean. I passed RV hook-ups with their gravel and asphalt. I pitched my tent in an open space with a firepit and a picnic table.

It had been an easy walk into the park, so as soon as my camp was organized, I followed signage for a nature walk through the campground. Trees and shrubs had identifying tags. I wished I was better at remembering how fir and hemlock differed. What evergreen huckleberry looked like in the wild. The name of that other shrub I'd already forgotten.

Near the end of the nature trail I saw a sign for the hiker biker camp. It was lovely—deep in the forest. It had cozy alcoves soft with pine needles and a locker for overnighting food.

I went back to the meadow-like spot where I'd camped and rolled up my tent. I carried it in a big, floppy bundle along the narrow path. A corner of the rainfly trailing behind me snagged on the shrubs. I felt silly making three trips into the forest from the open meadow, which I now realized was a group camp site. Mark would have explored before he set up. Why was I so impulsive?

As I searched for a stone for pounding stakes into the hard ground under the pine needles, I mounted a silent defense of myself. I would never be as careful as Mark. I would always make this kind of mistake. I had so much going on in my head, I was prone to tuning out the physical world, where he'd been so at home. But I could do well enough. Choosing the wrong campground—having to troop three times through the campground carrying my bundles to get it right—it was a small mistake. I could let myself make them often, learning to make decisions like this by myself.

The day had turned overcast. I devised a way to drape the tarp over my tent, sending thanks back to Ahnjayla again. For supper, I pulled out my cold leftover Pad Thai.

But I didn't have rain. Only, after I'd crawled under the tarp and into my tiny abode, a raccoon. I heard it rustling around with the lunch fixings I'd forgotten in a zippered flap at the top of my pack. My flashlight found his yellow eyes under the table. "Shoo!" I said, and waved the light. The eyes blinked off and then on again, unimpressed.

Falling asleep, *Four Strong Winds* came back to my mind from the hippie cafe. Winds blow lonely and won't change what I wanted changed. I wasn't even walking into my new life. I was only seeing the shape of one. I would make my way, impulsive and absent-minded. Mark would not be there to rescue me. Nothing too much would change, but I would get used to it. And was I really alone? For moments at a time lately, I'd known I would be happy again someday.

In the morning, I surveyed the invasion under my table. The raccoon had finished off my crackers, snapped open my air-tight box and eaten my peanut butter. Not on the crackers, I assumed. My bag of GORP was missing entirely, maybe taken home to the family. He—or maybe *she*, foraging for her kits—had bitten a hole in the sandwich bag holding my expensive sharp Irish cheddar. But left it behind. If I had to share, that seemed an acceptable division.

My hike that day was to walk over one of the lava-flow headlands on the Oregon Coast. Signs warned, BEAR COUNTRY. I walked with my bear spray in my hand. Even better, if the bears, as advertised, disliked surprises more than they disliked me, I would let them know I was coming. The hippie café had gotten me started on old favorites.

I sang Nevills Brothers, like their free bird on the wire. I sang Paul

Simon's ode to Mardi Gras several times, full of my joy in the silent green forest. I tried to remember all the verses of Elvis's *You Were Always on My Mind*, a song of endings. Full of regret.

There were things I could have said to Mark, things I could have done and hadn't. I stumbled along the narrow path until I came to a tree, slimmer than me but sturdy. It leaned oceanward on the downhill side of the path, smooth and light-barked. I lay flat against it and sobbed. Mark hadn't always treated me as well as he should have, hadn't loved me as I wished, but I truly had been always on his mind.

The trunk pressed hard against my breastbone, its raspy bark against my cheek. How could something so silent be such a comfort? I pulled myself together and went on. At a wide spot on the trail, still about five hundred feet above the ocean, a rough-cut bench was anchored into the hillside. I shucked off the pack and sat. To the north, the point of Cape Lookout tapered off into the distant gently-rocking sea. To the south, the coming headlands were far and dim and blue.

I closed my eyes and prayed my releasing prayers—my craving for safety and security, for power and control. Especially the aching need for love. I teased my mind again and again from regret into quiet. By the end of twenty minutes, when I opened my eyes, the sea, the headlands, the forest around me looked like they'd been through a cleansing rain.

That was the last time full-body sobs overtook me. When I fell against the tree and it held me, I finally stopped asking, *What will become of me?*

Signage had given me the impression the descent would be steep, but the headlands all seemed to have the same pattern: after a steep northern ascent, a gentler southern slope. I reached the beach and rested, waiting for the tide to head back out and give me solid sand to walk on.

Several hours later, I walked the beach until I found Galloway

Road. I followed the road to Sand Lake. No longer in a forest, with all its mulchy smells and shade, this campground offered only sand and a few scrubby coastal pines. Dunes dotted with sprays of sea grass stretched inland. I'd read that during the summer the dunes swarm with ATVs—the beer-belly demographic and their teenaged sons—but now it lay silent and mostly empty. The grass waved ever so slightly in the off-shore breeze.

High thin clouds to the east turned pink and orange, reflecting the setting sun. I had left my tarp folded up because the evening was clear. But as I ate supper, I looked south. Dark wisps were blowing in. Before the dusk faded into dark, I jerry-rigged the tarp as a lean-to from a low, leaning tree trunk to the ground at the foot of my tent. I stood back and smiled. As long as rain came from the south, I'd be fine. Mark would have laughed at my efforts, but would have been secretly proud of my try.

I was drifting to sleep when a huge crack of thunder startled me. The tarp rattled in a gusty wind. Lightning flashed. I counted to ten. The thunder crashed again, so loud I couldn't believe the storm could be ten miles away.

More thunder, and that rattly wind. Nine. Eight. At six, the rain started. The tent and the tarp were dead still now, but rain was falling harder and the storm moved closer until lightning and thunder were only four counts apart. Then it started to move away again. I stopped counting at thirteen and went to sleep.

Chapter 21

In the morning, only the trees were still dripping. I was surrounded in mist. I sat in the dry sand at the opening of my lean-to, thanked Ahnjayla again, and ate my granola. My camp smelled of clean sand. I packed up and set out full of energy and enthusiasm.

Sand Lake is an estuary that opens into the ocean. Bonnie Henderson recommended walking across the mouth of the lake at low tide, but her experience was no recommendation at all. She had missed low tide by only an hour. She *managed* to find a place to cross by searching inland, a place that was *barely shallow enough* to get across *without swimming or falling in*. She opined the worst thing that would happen if you fell was wet gear.

My imagination served up something much worse than wet gear. By this time, I had learned how I felt about deep water with a pack on my back. I'd faced it at Hug Point and crossing Nehalem Bay in a rowboat without a life jacket. Now, wading the mouth of the lake felt like something that would end up with me lying on the sandy lake floor, held there by my heavy pack, helpless as an upturned beetle.

I opted for a long detour around the lake. The back road was deserted on that off-season morning. The gravely verge, too narrow to be called a shoulder, sloped down into drainage ditches. Between several apple trees on the edge of a mowed yard, I saw a home. I stood and thought about picking an apple from a tree with its rosy crop just ready to drop. My overly earnest ethical compass told me that taking two apples would be theft, but one would be neighborly sharing, even if I didn't ask.

The apple was juicy and warmed by the sun. I thought of John

Markum and the feral apple tree in an abandoned meadow where he harvested the yearly supply of winter apples we'd eaten with our pork chops. Someday there'd be such a mix left behind if humans disappeared. The wild and the domesticated would live side by side and become each other. In the meantime, what if it's true that the world is designed to give us the basics we need?

I turned right, onto Highway 131, at a pole-barn auto repair and a bait shop. From there, the road went on and on past dairy farms. One breeze brought the sweet smell of drying hay and another wafted in with the smell of hay from the other end of cows.

Our farm in Salem had lain to the south of an organic dairy, where the hay fields were irrigated from the bubbling manure lagoons. Sprinklers shot water and odor into the air in huge arcs during the dry summer months. Kenny had called that section of the road Brown Water Curves.

When I finally walked into the town of Tierra Del Mar, I cut over a small dune and back to the ocean. It was a relief to walk on sand again, to smell salt, to hear the constant rush of the tide and feel the interplay of warm sunshine and a cool breeze. To have busy sea bird companions.

But three hours on the gritty asphalt of back roads had worn me out. My shoulders were cramping, my feet hurt, and I was walking into a headwind. My long detour had landed me back on the beach near high tide. The waves' foamy edges kept eating up the hard-packed sand and pushing me higher, into sand with no traction.

I trudged forward. I prayed. I thought again about how good it was for me to be making all the big and small daily decisions. Back home, would I still notice what I wanted, what I needed? I'd so disregarded myself in the rough and tumble of marriage and children. Maybe if I went to Ethiopia, maybe if I lived in remotest Maji, where I grew up, there would be hope that I'd learn to hang onto my own steering.

I was once again on a section of beach where vehicles are allowed. Tire tracks crisscrossed the sand and disappeared at the edge of the tide. For a few minutes, I was distracted from my fatigue by a pick-up stuck in the soft sand. The driver, a man, was spinning his wheels, shooting sand out behind the truck like a yellow rooster tail. The pickup sank lower. A woman was standing off to the side. Her posture suggested she'd been talked into this idea of fun. What had she given up to be there—a chat over coffee with friends? A curl-up on the couch with an interesting memoir? Or was that just me I was projecting?

Eventually, nothing could distract me. My feet ached. The pack pulled against my shoulders. My quads burned. At any time, they might just refuse to lift and I would stand rooted in the sand like Lot's wife, turned to salt. What would happen to me if I actually couldn't go on? An emergency vehicle. Mortification. Surely, I could keep going. I leaned forward, into the wind so that I would fall if I didn't put my foot out for another step. Another. I counted my footsteps. I counted to one hundred. And to one hundred again.

Ahead of me was still the climb up Cape Kiwanda, a headland entirely different from the others, its sandstone formed millions of years ago, when the West Coast was part of the ocean floor. There are fossils in the sand and mudstone—even, in one place, the fossil of a whale.

Weirdly, another basalt haystack-shaped rock stands in the ocean at the tip of the cape. Geologists think the lava penetrated the sandstone, flowed under the surface, and erupted again out in the ocean. The basalt has protected the sandstone from wave action. But now, wave and wind have reduced the basalt and erosion is speeding up on Cape Kawanda.

Off the beach, the cape has atomized into a sand dune 240 feet high. I stood, panting, at the foot of the dune: soft sand all the way up.

A signpost fifty feet above the beach on the steep dune warned *No Motorized Vehicles*. How fear-blind people with ATVs would have to be to try it! I guessed how many footsteps it would take me to get to the sign, and started up, counting. When I got to the sign, I threw my pack down and dropped beside it. The sand was warm. I wiggled myself a cradle, and shaded my eyes with my sweaty arm. When I finally gathered enough strength to sit up, I dug out cheese and crackers. The biker at my first campground in Fort Stevens had told me—what on earth had we been talking about?—that Canadians eat jam on their cheese. I ripped open a packet of jam I'd kyped from a café, and ate my cheese and crackers *a la* Canadienne.

Once I'd rested and eaten, I managed the remaining climb. At the top I shook out my ponytail and lifted my face to the breeze. I'd made it through my hardest day yet. I took a step off the peak and slid, laughing, five feet. It felt like skiing must feel, a sport I'd missed, growing up in Ethiopia. Swoosh, swoosh, swoosh, I slid into civilization in Pacific City, population 1,027.

The shape of the headland and its protective rock both channel the wind and waves across the beach, not into it. A dory fleet sets out from Pacific City, and people come just to watch them go out and return to land. The town hosts windsurfing and kite flying competitions. In spite of being off-season, the beach that day was swarming. Wind surfers wrestled their bright sails and their audience milled around in brighter swimsuits.

And everyone eats at Pelican Pub, right there at the base of the dune. I stumbled in, set my companionable pack in the booth beside me, asked the server if she would plug in my phone, and ordered clam chowder. I had an hour before the bus came by to take me past the next road-walk to a campground.

Blood thrummed along my legs on the banquette, resupplying my big muscles with oxygen. Sand crunched in my shoes. Sand itched along my hairline. Grains of sand nestled at the base of every hair on my arms. My face felt crusty from my sweat and the salt in the air. I smelled the sun and wind on my skin.

The bus that hopped me around Nestucca Bay cost two dollars. Two men chatting in seats ahead of me agreed that by the look of boats out on the rivers, the salmon must be running. Another said his son had caught a twenty-five pounder that week.

The bus driver dropped me at a narrow road leading to Winema Beach, which stretches along the tiny, seldom-visited town of Neskowin. I had a room reserved there in the only hotel, and supper planned with a friend who was teaching in the town's tiny private school.

The ocean was at high tide. I was going to have to wait, or face more wading through shifty sand. The waves were noisy and manically restless. I leaned against a log, facing Cascade Head to the south, blue in the mist. I was still tired, and wanted to sleep for a few minutes, but the sand was damp so I just sat there.

I dug around in my pack and found the tiny New Testament in a modern English paraphrase that I'd tucked into a corner. The faux leather cover curved under my thumbs. The print was tiny, the pages so thin they should have been translucent. I flipped them, looking. In the gospel of Matthew, right near the beginning, I found the beatitudes.

I'd memorized hundreds of verses for Bible classes in boarding school. I'd learned this one as, *Come unto me, all ye who are weary and heavy burdened, and I will give you rest.* The modern translation startled me: *Get away with me and you'll recover your life....Learn the unforced rhythms of grace...learn to live freely and lightly.*

At the moment, I was too tired for anything but unforced rhythms. I closed the book and held it on my lap. Did I have two selves? A yammering, frightened, grasping self and a peaceful, graceful self? Maybe admitting the first I would discover the other, uncovering it and letting it grow.

Chapter 22

When the high tide receded, I hoisted the pack up. I began talking out loud in Amharic on the wide, empty beach. Even with months between visits to Ethiopia, somehow Amharic stayed in my mind. People there would ask, *AlTuffashhim? Hasn't it been lost to you?* For a few days after I arrived in Addis Ababa, some words would float just out of reach until I heard someone else use them, and then they would drop back into my stream of available vocabulary. Often, mysteriously, I discovered I had mastered some new twist of grammar during my time away. As though my brain had its own ways of learning in unforced rhythms, free of grammar books and dictionaries.

I had said to Miriam that I should probably figure out whether I wanted to find a new partner before I went off to Maji. "Who would find me there?"

She laughed. "Oh Mom! You know there would be plenty of men in Ethiopia willing to find you!"

It was true. Ethiopians are famous for their belief that America truly is the land flowing with milk and honey, the land *where dollars are like leaves.* Why wouldn't people back in Ethiopia think that, when their immigrant relatives send dollars back to support the family? The USA for them was a land worth doing anything at all to get to.

I'd watched an Ethiopian teacher friend leave her husband, children, and two-month-old baby to skip her tourist visa and disappear into the Little Addis Ababa community in Atlanta. She'd undoubtedly found a way to get citizenship and then sent for her whole family, to reunite them in a new world.

I'd had young adults beg me to adopt them—*you speak Amharic and I'm* kai, *light-skinned!* Miriam was right: I would represent a U.S. passport to men who considered themselves eligible. And really, does love follow a plan that I could figure out ahead?

My friend and a friend of hers joined me for supper in Neskowin's one restaurant. My tongue stumbled over the words to answer their questions and I felt embarrassed. My social skills had slipped. I couldn't say how my pilgrimage was going. It was both wonderful and just a trudge. And the deeper answer she was looking for...I couldn't explain all that I was seeing and not seeing. All that I was learning but not yet understanding about who my self was going to be in the new life I was looking for.

I hadn't been able to explain the grief itself, either. I had tried to tell my sisters, but later, as they lost their husbands one by one, each said to me, *I thought I understood. Now I do.* Now, in Neskowin, words let me down when I tried to explain my halting, erratic recovery. A guy wire had snapped with Mark's death. My life stood leaning. Pilgrimage was my hope for finding new sources of balance. Maybe it was happening. Slowly.

I changed the subject. I sat back to enjoy the hot food. I listened to the two of them chat, leaning toward each other, their faces alight. I wanted to remember again how to do that.

In the comfort of my hotel room that evening, I sat with my journal. I tried to peer into my future—now that I was more than halfway through with my pilgrimage, it should be solidifying. I was still awash in myths about destiny, predestination, and the notion of time extending like a line from the fog of the past into the fog of the future. As though the future is hard to see, but it's there if you look intently enough. For two weeks, I had been looking intently. But what I was seeing, barely taking shape in the fog, was that the steps on the way create the future. There is nothing to see until we get there.

I thought again about Ethiopia. Just as Mark was dying, I'd heard again from a high school friend who was working in Uganda, helping rural Africans get access to electricity. It seemed like a sign. I would like to work for a nonprofit like his. Was I too old? I asked God about Ethiopia. Again, the answer was neither yes or no. What was coming downstream to me would be the answer.

I read my tattered pages of wisdom from David Whyte. He taught curiosity, fascination for seeing who I am in my new situation. He said to notice how people see me, how I affect them and they affect me.

Who had I been a year ago; who had I become in the year since Mark died? Who would I be next? Maybe I could join a hiking club and write about the OCT. I could get good at the waltz, the foxtrot, the cha cha. I could take lessons and practice in the kitchen as I cooked for myself. I could develop friendships with both men and women in the dance community.

My sister had met an editor with a Master's degree in African Studies. I could hire her to coach me on the memoir about my life in Ethiopia, Kenya, and South Sudan that I had been writing and re-writing for at least ten years—I would do that. I had a consulting job lined up for that winter, but I didn't think it would lead to anything more. It didn't feel like my destiny, whatever that is. I put lots of question marks around *Development Work*. And I wrote that I would no longer think of myself as a widow, but as a single woman. There seemed to be a big difference in my mind between those words. And I hadn't been a single woman since the year I was twenty.

Late that evening, I closed my eyes and prayed my releasing prayers—letting go of those needs that felt so urgent. I also released Mark from having been a husband any different than he had been, or having not died but having stayed with me. I wondered if I should release myself from any further obligation to him.

I released the farm, and gave thanks for the years there that were so rich with work that anchored me on the earth, with chicks and apples, seedlings and compost. I released the house that gave Mark projects, gave me space for a huge desk, gave us room for our grown kids to land with their spouses during times of transition. That house, which could hold all my siblings plus the Portland cousins for Thanksgiving dinners. And that house, sold, which was giving me money to live on until I could find a new job or claim social security.

Then I committed again to waiting. I needed to let new work come to me. I needed to wait and see whether to look for another partner. I hoped, as David Whyte had assured, that I would know the right decision—I might even by then be living it.

Before I went to bed, I checked the plan for Lincoln City, where I was headed next. I had to take a bus again, around the back of Cascade Head, where the trail hadn't yet been cleared of fallen trees from a storm the year before.

By the time the bus picked me up, the wind was high, whipping my hair around and dropping big splats of rain in my face. The scent of rain on dust overrode the scent of bacon and coffee that had clung to my clothes in Neskowin's one cafe.

I paid and asked the bus driver if he could drop me off at the Devil's Lake Campground. He was gruff: *The bus stops at Safeway, turns around and goes back up the coast.*

Lincoln City is a long strip of a town, only a few blocks wide along both sides of Highway 101. Even in a car, the town seems to go on forever. I had never noticed a Safeway. Walking through Lincoln City to Devil's Lake would be my trek for the day.

As we drove, the rain began in earnest. I watched the bus's windshields smack back and forth as we rolled south. The rain was supposed to have held off until afternoon. *Oh well,* I thought. *This will be over by the time I get to Lincoln City.*

I got off at Safeway and huddled in the bus stop shelter to wait out the rain that was now pelting down. After a while, I thought there must be something I could buy inside Safeway, where it would be warmer. I walked slowly through the aisles and finally chose some grapes. I couldn't keep wandering around—I wasn't inconspicuous. I shivered. My wet wool sweater had lost any capacity for insulating me and the store felt air conditioned, stuck in summer mode.

I paid and stepped back outside. I walked back and forth under the little shopping center's overhanging roof, watching the rain. It ebbed and surged like the tide, not so far away. Finally, I thought there was a bit of a break. I put up the hood of my sweater and cinched the pack up tight.

There had not been any real break in the rain, only a few seconds of lull between gusts. Rain on my glasses refracted shades of gray concrete, asphalt and mist. There was hardly any traffic. Under a Farmers Insurance office awning, I huddled against the wall, out of sight from the windows, waiting for the next lull.

How far was Devil's Lake? I had no idea. Distance measured in driving time was no use to me on foot. How would I get the tarp up over my flimsy tent in this driving rain when I got there? Would there be any trees to tie it to in the campground? Would anything in my pack be dry by the time I got set up? I couldn't even sit in the tent—how would I eat?

The weather took a breath. I dashed to the awning of a real estate office a quarter of a block away. I had to be alert to even notice the lulls in rain. They may have only been my imagination. Plastered against my forehead, my bangs dripped water onto my eyelashes. The sodden hem of my sweater hung low. It bumped and slapped against my legs.

Finally, up a rise, I saw a sign for the Captain Cook Inn. Vacancy, bright red, glowed through the blowing rain. *Yes, please.*

Their Deluxe Queen wasn't all that deluxe, but it was dry. My t-shirt stuck to me as I peeled it off. My socks dripped on the floor of the bathroom as I dropped them in a wet pile beside my underpants. The bathwater, hot as I could tolerate, raised goosebumps on my arms and legs and I shivered.

I lay back and closed my eyes. I rocked my knees up and down slightly, just enough to send the water over my shoulders. My hair floated around my neck. I didn't try to think further than *Thank you!* for Captain Cook and the hotelier he had inspired in Lincoln City.

When the bathwater began to cool, I washed my hair. I stood, and felt a little light-headed. I stepped out. My foot slipped. My body hit the tile. The corner of the baseboard heater along the wall gouged into my back.

I lay for a minute on the cold floor. Then I grabbed onto the toilet seat to pull myself up. I stood, leaning against the sink, shaking. If I had hit my head, how long before someone would have missed me? Would Kenny have tried calling? Would the hotel manager have wondered? I could also fall at home. This could be my future. I wouldn't see it coming. No one would know.

I shook off the urge to scare myself. I patted the blood off my shoulder blade with toilet paper, which melted in my fingers and floated red in the toilet.

Chapter 23

In the small room at the Captain Cook Inn, I draped wet clothes over every surface. I checked my back again in the mirror and wiped off a few more spots of seeping blood. I plugged my phone in and crawled into the soft, warm bed. No bed had ever seemed more of a nest, more of a refuge.

By morning, the top of my sweater was dry but gravity had pulled the remaining gallon of rain water to the bottoms of the sleeves, the hem, the hood. I squeezed them over the bathtub and hung them back up. I pulled my granola out of the food bag and ate while I looked up the weather. Rain for a week, all up and down the coast.

I had turned down my sister's good backpacking tent because it was heavier than the flimsy nylon pup tent. Now, even if I could bear walking onward to Florence in the rain, how would I get dry and warm again every day? And how would I get through cold wet nights?

I snuggled back in the bed with a bunch of pillows against my back. I got suddenly mad. I hadn't finished my pilgrimage. The choice was being taken away from me.

My thinking shifted slowly away from blaming fate. My planning had been as flimsy as my tent, full of superstition and as though I could control things no one can control. I'd wanted to walk as close to the end of a full year since Mark died as possible. I'd assumed the rain would hold off, just because I wanted it to. I would have my enlightened moments in the wild. Then I'd arrive at the magic threshold and I would step over it at last.

I'd waited until too late. I felt scared now, seeing how vulnerable I really was, how out of control of circumstances, how misguided in my thinking.

I called Cathy. She made sympathetic murmuring noises, and tears sprang into my eyes, breaking through the numbness I had felt since I'd picked myself up off the bathroom floor. I told her I would give myself another day at the Captain Cook Inn to dry my things out. Then would she meet me at the bus station in Portland?

As Cathy and I turned onto my street, the tiny rental house looked foreign and desolate, the yard littered with brown and yellow leaves, the windows blank.

Cathy lugged my pack out of her trunk. "Every time you come back to this house and feel a jolt of joy, it will seem more and more like your home."

I doubted it. I didn't say anything.

I threw every stitch of my walking wardrobe into the washer. I called to make an appointment for a massage. Then I walked down the street to Cathy's house for supper. I told some of my stories to her and her husband and we laughed. I felt high. I walked back in my warm dry clothes in the chilly dusk to what could become my home. It seemed possible to begin my new life.

The next day, I called each of my boys. I thought about Miriam, eleven time zones away in Kenya. I played my guitar until my tender fingers were sore, and wrote an email to a friend. The house settled quiet and chilly around me.

I'd done so much grieving. I'd been a good sport. Maybe there wasn't a magical threshold. And the gray zone would go on longer than I could bear. Such a bitter promise. I sank into a new layer of sadness. I really didn't have any idea how to go on. I really did have to do it without Mark. All my walking, all my making the best of being alone on the OCT, weren't going to bring back that good life. *The one*, I thought regretfully, *that I didn't fully appreciate when it spread so comfortably around me.* I was still hanging onto false hope. Seeing through it for a moment and then falling again and again into the dream that I could get back what I'd lost.

When my masseur's hands touched my back, they felt like food, water, breath. How long it had been since my flesh had felt tender touch. I wept silently, my eyes closed and my tears falling through the headrest to the floor below. I hoped he wouldn't notice and ask if I was okay. I was, in the most essential way, but I couldn't have said yes.

I tried to bring my mood up the next day by walking mail over to the friend I was renting the house from. She was in her yard, putting her garden to bed for the winter. She asked if I was doing better. I wasn't. Not yet. She led me into the house and made me a cup of tea. She asked about Jesse and Beth, and I told her about their miscarriage. We both buried our faces in the steam wafting up from our cups. There seemed no end of sadness.

I walked home, thinking about October the year before. Mark had been drifting in a morphine haze, wasting away. I'd been jolting awake nights when he paused between breaths. I'd been making him the ice chips he'd ask for because he couldn't manage even a straw. They would melt away as he drifted off again. I was dumping his catheter bag. Knocking him out with Lorazepam when he hallucinated. Maybe Octobers were just going to be hard for a while.

I told myself that in two years I would feel different. I stopped and gave the thought serious consideration. Yes, it felt true. In two years, I would absolutely be over the worst of the raw spots. I could count on being happier more of the time. *Something will have changed by then*, I thought. *You can make it through two years.* Then I prayed my releasing prayers and let the future breathe.

In the near future, I was going to Ethiopia. My Ethiopian friends in Maji had asked why didn't I step in to coordinate the Bible translation team when the present coordinator left? I didn't know that local language. I'd never been involved in translation. But they'd asked. Maybe they just needed someone with a Calvinist big-sister ability to organize and encourage. I would talk to the folks at the translation headquarters in Addis Ababa about that. I would visit Miriam and her family in Nairobi for Christmas.

When I walked back into the little house that still felt strange to me, I sat down to meditate. I opened my eyes. Calm and clear again, I was ready to start planning that next trip. I looked up airports where I could connect with Ethiopian Airlines: Washington DC, Toronto, Frankfort, Amsterdam.

And then, right next to the list of airports and airfare options in my journal, I started listing the towns and state parks south of Lincoln City: Beverly Beach, Newport, South Beach, Ona Beach, Waldport. Beachside, Yachats, Cape Perpetua, Washburne, Sutton Lake. What was left of my walk was what I had hoped the whole trail would be like—a stretch of unbroken days nature walking, with campgrounds within about eight miles of each other.

My mind had submitted to the reasonable, the inevitable. But my body was researching options.

I looked up the weather. Rain on the coast was going to lift. I was a hiker now. I was a backpacker. I didn't yet need to coop myself up for the winter. There was sunshine to be had on the coast.

In a surge of excitement, I went to REI to buy gas for my little stove. I called my backpacking sister to borrow her rain-ready tent. I quoted Buddha in my journal: *Seawater always tastes like salt; enlightenment always feels like freedom.* I meditated, prayed my prayers. I reached for trust and joy.

I curled up on the loveseat where Mark and I had watched movies together. In my journal from early October the year before, I had written how sure I was that Mark would die on the tenth. That's how I wanted the story to line up—he would die exactly five months from his diagnosis on June tenth. I wanted the corners of my life, about to spin out of control, to be square and even.

By the end of that September, I had told people that Mark was near the end. His sister came to Bend to say good-bye. My sister Janie came and listened to my pronouncement doubtfully. She said he looked like he might still have time left. He did have not days, but exactly a month.

I read again in my journal about crawling into bed with Mark in the hospice hospital. I had slipped one arm behind him. I held his thin hand with my other, his fingers so long and blunt and now all bone and tendons. He said, *I feel so much more at peace when you're here.* Then he drifted back to sleep, and I stayed where I was, unwilling to disturb him by moving, wondering who would hold me when it was my turn.

But later that day, Mark had said he thought he should get out of bed and try to pee.

I said, "Do you actually need to?"

He was having so much trouble walking even to his little bathroom that he would often sit on the bed for a half hour or longer, before he could stand. "It's good for me to."

I asked him if that was really true.

He snapped, "Don't try to micromanage me. Soon enough I'll be in a coma and you can run things however you want."

I started to cry. I finally managed to say, "All your life you've lived with *shoulds*. I want you to be free. If it feels good to move, then do it. But if there's just some big category of things that you *should do* because they're good for you—that's not enough reason anymore."

He sat on the edge of the bed for a while longer, then crawled back in.

At the hospice hospital that day, something deep inside me had begun to unhook from Mark. He would leave. He was right, I would go on. I would continue to be pretty much who I'd always been. I'd still be someone who would find interesting things to do. I'd have a good life going forward. However, glimpsing the truth doesn't make it easier to live into.

My kids had watched me, worried, as October tenth, the day I had said Mark would die, neared. He was still hanging on. They were afraid that I would fall apart on October eleventh. But I handled it a lot like I handled the hard hiking days. When I got tired on the trail, I made up deadlines, timelines, endings. I convinced myself I could make it this far; now that far. Even in the loose sand trying to reach Kiwanda Head, I had found inside myself the conviction that I could go *that* much further. Even when the end was further yet, I found more strength than I thought I had.

Back when Mark was nearing death, to get to October tenth I had pulled up all the strength I thought I had. I still had twenty more days to go. I didn't know it then. But I found my strength had not yet run out.

And on the day I'd thought Mark should die, I opened my journal and wrote, *This time will not go on forever. It won't be easier on the other side, so don't be impatient. You don't want to be left with guilt and regret that you wasted or hurried these last days. Don't wish them away. These moments will be part of you forever.*

I didn't make a reasoned decision to take up my pilgrimage again and bring it to a more orderly end. I didn't try to figure out why I wanted to go back out. I didn't set goals or attach desired outcomes. I just kept getting ready. The day before weather on the Coast was supposed to clear, I organized the backpack again. There was a dance convention in Portland that weekend. Kenny called to tell me, and asked if I wanted to join him.

Between dances, a friend asked me how my kids were doing, missing Mark. I hadn't heard much from them lately. I said, "I don't really know, here comes Kenny, let's ask."

"It's getting more intermittent," he said. "But the grief is still around."

The three of us tapped our feet to the music and talked. A net of small joys in that moment held me. Small joys would always surface and lift me higher than seemed reasonable.

At 2:30 in the morning, Kenny said his feet were killing him, was I ready to go? We changed our shoes and reached for our coats. But then *Layla* came on, so swingy, so smitten, so obsessed—Eric Clapton belting out his passion for George Harrison's wife.

"One more!" I pulled him back up. "You can dance in sneakers!"

He laughed, that I still had spunk in the middle of the night, that I was still learning new things. "How old are you, sixty-two?"

"Sixty-four. And a half."

"No way! No way!"

When I said I wanted to be a good enough dancer to be a fun partner, he said, "You're there already. You're not heavy to move around the floor. Not stiff or awkward." He said when I got my spins locked down, that would make a big difference. "If I've got a complicated string put together, you're not quite getting all the way around in time for me to lead into it."

I said I was thinking of cutting my hair, but he said I should keep it long. "Don't try to look young. Your ponytail and braid look retro. Which is good, because—*you're* retro."

I had told Jesse on the phone that I thought I needed to wait, not go rushing off to look for another partner. He had been sad. Kenny was too, when I told him. I thought they'd be relieved not to have to deal with a new man in the family. I saw now that they wanted me to be happy.

I told Kenny that I'd poked around on Match.com. I think he was surprised there were people in my demographic doing that. But hadn't yet signed up, I needed to wait. To wait at least until I went back to Ethiopia. In spite of Miriam's kidding about eager husband applicants there, in spite of my nagging loneliness, my waiting until after a trip to Ethiopia was only partly about finding a partner. It was also because I needed something big to do. Something that would soak up the energy and gifts I still had in me. Something to give me meaning. Something I, myself, could do in my alone strength.

I drove home from the dance with Kenny, tired and happy, quietly held by love.

Chapter 24

On a bus to the Tillamook hub, I slept off my late-night dance. I would catch the NW Connector in Tillamook, and it would take me to where I'd been headed a week earlier, before rain drove me off the OCT. I woke with the rocking of the bus as it rounded the block to the station. I had a stiff neck. But excitement overrode my discomfort—I would sleep outside again that night. I stepped out of the bus and into a clear day on the coast, with brush-stroke clouds and a cool breeze.

With an hour to wait for my connection, I trundled myself and my pack from the bus station into downtown Tillamook again. Sure enough, my sun hat had become part of the clutter in the 2nd Street Café. There it hung from a vintage coat rack, with an assortment of scarves and sweaters. I didn't explain or ask, just ordered a latte and walked out with coffee and my hat. I smiled on my way back to the bus station. How pleased frugal Mark would have been that I'd retrieved it. How little it took for me to feel competent and in control of my life again.

A young woman with a pack like mine sat with her back against the station wall. She carried a small instrument case, maybe a clarinet, and was wearing hiking boots and a turquoise mesh skirt, another version of my hiking skirt and boots. What a motley collection of humanity we were, with our strange clothes and our dreams and sorrows, drawn to the ocean.

The bus dropped me off at Beverly Beach State Park, south of Lincoln City. I breathed deeply the clean moist air of salt water and sand. But setting up camp, my back seized up. I straightened. It twinged whenever I turned my torso or bent down. I moved carefully, taking out food, tightening the tiny heating unit onto my new cannister of fuel, heating water for my freeze-dried supper. I ate slowly at the picnic table.

The next morning, I decided the intermittent spasms were from dancing. Or from sitting, sitting, sitting, feeling glum in my house in Portland. Not from walking. I dug out the one med I'd squirreled away after Mark's illness—prescription strength Aleve that a hospice doctor had given him long after Aleve was doing him any good. I broke camp gingerly, and started out. Walking felt good.

I had overcast skies for the long walk from Beverly Beach to South Beach State Park. After I crossed on the shoulder of the Yaquina Bay Bridge south of Newport, rain began.

How could the weatherman let me down like this? I climbed up a little knoll and leaned against a fir, settling into the deep nest of needles.

The tree sheltered me for a while. Cars passed on the road below, their wipers on *intermittent*. After about an hour, cars were wiping their windshields steadily and the tree was dripping on me. I got out the thin plastic poncho I'd brought, opened its neat little packet and arranged it over both me and the pack leaning beside me. I got out my bag of GORP.

Eventually, I got chilled. The rain was showing no signs of letting up. If I set out in it, would I warm up walking, or just get wetter and colder? I wouldn't have a hot bath or a cushy bed to snuggle down in that night at South Beach. On the other hand, the poncho would keep my sweater dry. And surely, I would come to a restaurant or a motel.

I struggled to get the pack on and the poncho over it. As I stepped back out onto the road's shoulder, the wind was in my face. I couldn't tell if the water drenching my legs was from rain or from the spray of cars zipping by. A mile is a long way, on foot in the rain. My body heat, as I walked as fast as I could, condensed moisture on the inside of the poncho. My clothes felt clammy. Finally, finally, a burger and seafood restaurant showed up over a rise in the road.

I ducked in, grateful for the dim light as I stood in the doorway, letting my eyes adjust. The poncho dripped on the mat.

I chose a booth away from the door, but not too close to the bar and the few people perched on stools. I pushed the damp pack into the corner and slipped in beside it. Hoping no one would notice me, I dug out my one change of clothes and slunk over to the restroom.

When I got settled again, deliciously dry in my pajama tights and t-shirt and doubly grateful for the dim lighting, I ordered hot chocolate and a salmon omelet.

"Are you the person I saw huddled under a poncho?" the waitress asked. "I was driving to work. I said to myself, 'I hope that person is okay.'" She came back to give me a hot chocolate refill. She said I could hang out there as long as I needed to. I looked up at her, amazement and thanks hopefully showing on my face, thinking again of Ahnjayla. I had never before put myself so often in this kind of vulnerable position. I had never given myself the chance to see how much grace is embedded in the kindness of strangers that my mother had taught me to scorn.

I charged my phone and looked up the weather. There was supposed to be a break in the rain from 2-5:00 and then a twenty percent chance through the night. The next day, twenty percent again, and then nothing for the rest of the week.

I sipped the hot chocolate refill and wrote in my journal. Earlier that morning, I had come to one of those beach streams that trickle out of the bluff where land gives way to sand. It spread out wide, hurrying to lose itself with all its sister water in the ocean. Up from me stood a cairn, one large upright stone with another balanced on it, marking the best place to ford. Someone had thought about the unknown hikers who would come after them. David Whyte's philosophical riffs had admonished me to notice the unseen support we all get from the earth, from our ancestors, from strangers.

As I lumbered from stone to stone across the stream, I had thought of the deep forests, each tree one of thousands. They protected each other from the wind. One tree doesn't collapse because its neighbor has fallen. Each has its own place and time.

And then, the tree that does fall becomes soil again. Tiny saplings grow in a row in the pithy trough that had once been a tree—nursery logs, they're called. The rhythm of death and renewal in the forest. A fallen tree nurtures others with its own heartwood.

The sign over the restaurant door had said *burgers*, but the dim lighting suggested their bar was their main business. After 2:00, I walked over to a tiny window to confirm the weather prediction. It was wet but clear out on the road. I left a big tip and set out again in the chill moist air for the walk to South Beach State Park.

I got a little lost, looking for the park's driveway. Then I wandered, looking for the intake booth. I didn't know I had entered from the back. I was exhausted by the time I found the booth, where sign on the window told me to come back in ten minutes. Again, I wandered, losing the signage to the hiker-biker section over and over.

I limped back to pay after I got my sister's tent and my mattress set up. I couldn't stop myself from giving the ranger my feedback. "The signage to the hiker-biker camp was confusing. I know we don't pay as much, but we're the ones coming in exhausted and desperate to rest." And I just had to add, looking for some sympathy, "I got caught in the rain."

She was not a smiler. No sympathy was going to come from this department. "Why didn't you take the bus? Don't you have children?"

"I have three. They're grown. But I'm just paying for myself."

"Why didn't they stop you?"

I was shocked.

But neither of us had to practice social niceties, out there at the edge of the forest. If she wanted to know, I was perfectly willing to tell her. "My husband died this month last year. I'm walking to mark the end of the year without him."

She counted my change silently and handed it to me. "My husband and daughter were killed two years ago this month. I've never dealt with it."

I stood silent for a long moment, a cup struggling to hold what she'd poured. I slowly pocketed my change and the receipt. "Yeah. It's hard to figure out."

She glanced up into my eyes just for a second.

I stumbled back to my camp. We all face so much loss. We all do our best to go on.

I was grateful that night, eating my supper and going to bed in a tent I could sit up in. When it began to rain at 3:00 a.m., I was grateful again that it was waterproof. *Thank you.*

In the morning, I went to the hospitality center and made myself a cup of hot tea. It began to rain again. I cradled the hot paper cup and gave thanks. And I was utterly determined to go on. I didn't question my decision to come again to the coast. To walk for as long as I could. Portland had felt foreign, cold, empty. I wasn't ready to face the quiet house. Rain and fatigue gave me something to match myself against. Rain and fatigue brought to me people who were supportive with their ordinary humanness. I could let it show how much I felt on the edge, unbalanced, unable yet to be normal.

The rain never came down harder than a light drizzle, so eventually I packed up camp. Everything was either damp or fully wet. As I walked, I sang. Mom and Dad had taken a collection of records with them to Ethiopia, and in remote, no-grid Maji, Dad hooked up the record player to a truck battery that hulked under a card table in our dining room. He would play a record for us some nights as we fell asleep: Schubert's Unfinished Symphony; Rachmaninoff's piano concerto; Paul Robeson's deep baritone singing about the Old Man River and John Henry. *Sometimes I feel like a motherless child.*

Around midday, the sun came out. I came to the Seal Rock State Recreation Area, where drivers could pull in and sit on a wooden deck and benches to enjoy a view of the beach. I unpacked the tent and spread it out. There must have been at least a pound of water in the rain fly alone. I spread out a few damp clothes as well, wondering if I'd get chased away as a vagrant. But no one else came by. The tourist season was well past, now that rain had started.

The OCT onward was another walking stretch on Highway 101.

On a hunch, I took out Ahnjayla's bus schedule, now getting more and more tattered. Sure enough, there was a bus stop just down the road. I finished my lunch and packed up the dry things, warmed by the sun.

I found a place to sit near the bus stop, in front of the Yuzen Restaurant, which looked like it had been closed for a while. I shut my eyes and meditated. Sunlight shone densely warm on my face.

I paid one dollar to be dropped off at the driveway of the Waldport KOA. Because there were so few campers, the man in the KOA registration booth offered me a regular site up front for the same price as their primitive sites on the other side of the campground. It meant putting up my little backpacking tent in the lee of a large RV. But it also meant I was near the restrooms.

By late afternoon, the sky was clear, the sun was bright, my sleeping bag was completely dry, and I'd taken a shower. I sat at my picnic table and wondered if there really was anything left for me to learn on the trail. On the other hand, did everything have to edify me? Maybe I could practice enjoying. I loved sleeping sheltered from the natural night only by fabric. There would be more nights. There would be beaches. There would be this beautiful fall weather, the sun canted toward the south, traveling in its flattened arc over the sky.

I closed my eyes and shifted into meditation.

God is surely ironic. I had, there in the Newport KOA, the only vision I ever had in all my years of spiritual practice. I saw Mark's face—not a photo, which was all my memory seemed able to reconstruct. I saw Mark's face, real and contorting with anger because I was no longer focused on him. I stood up to him in my vision. I told him he had left and had no rights over me anymore.

When he disappeared, I started to cry.

I repeated my sacred word. I returned to quiet.

When twenty minutes were up, I opened my eyes. I was facing an empty playground. The sky was brilliant blue. The sun had dried my hair. From where I sat, I could see parts of the Art Deco Yaquina Bay bridge. I walked to the KOA overlook to see it more clearly, arches bounding over the deeply blue and teal waters of the bay, pillars tapering up and up against the sky. It was true, what the Medieval cathedral builders believed, that the lines of construction can lift our thoughts.

After supper at the picnic table in the shadow of the big RV, whose occupants I never saw, I walked to the bridge to watch the sun set. I went early, and stood on the bridge, waiting. The sun didn't seem in any hurry. I began to worry. The future I was walking toward was crammed with unknowns. How could I embrace so many?

A friend had suggested that I not imagine my first year without Mark as a hallway leading from the room with my former life to another new room. Instead, look at this corridor as a room of a different sort. This time, this transition, was my life. Live in it.

And David Whyte said just entering a conversation with the unknown will transform. Just ask the courageous questions and wait. I waited now for the sun to set, more willing to be patient.

In the west, the quarter moon hung in the sky, also ready to set. It brightened from white to silver against the edge of dark clouds on the horizon. The sun turned the entire sky behind them both to fire. Gilt-edged, the clouds waited quietly for the sun to pillow into them.

My future would unfold. I didn't have to create it. If I prayed for peace and joy, I would embrace the circumstances that would welcome them. Hope for their coming would bear my weight.

Chapter 25

That night, I woke in the KOA with my hip on the ground. My crinkly camp mat had sprung a slow leak. I rose in the dark, the moon long gone. I blew the mattress back up without opening my eyes. My determination was really being tested, the future again proving itself unknown and possibly uncomfortable.

In the morning, my tent dripped with dew and my mood was somber. Could I enjoy my last days of camping if I woke nights with my hip aching? I sat on the damp picnic bench with my things spread out around me, drying.

I had seen an electric outlet and a folding chair in the laundry room—they represented a phone call and a charged phone for the next day or two. But I hesitated. Wasn't I still on pilgrimage? Wasn't I raised to soldier on without needs? Suddenly I couldn't think what was noble about struggling alone. I'd been learning about kindness and help. Maybe a step toward contentment in my new singleness was *not* to do it alone. Maybe human contact of every kind is what we're here for. I set myself up in the laundry room and called a friend. We laughed together. My spirits lifted.

I packed up my tent that didn't leak and my mattress that did and set out again, walking the wide, lovely beach. Under an overcast sky, the ocean was pewter to the south, silver where the sun, heading west, began to reflect off it. To the north, the waves were gray and deep green. In constant, constant motion, the colors shifted and swirled into each other. No rest. My noisy companions, the billions of shapeless molecules crashing together, made a sound wholly out of proportion to their size.

After an easy beach walk, I found the Beachside campground

squeezed between the highway and the beach. RVs were strung out in two rows along the inland edge, and the tent camping area hugs so close to the ocean the brochure said it floods during super high tides. Bonnie Henderson had warned that Beachside State Park wasn't very exciting. That's because she hadn't stayed at the Newport KOA.

The surf hummed to me as I set up camp in a cul-de-sac among shore pines, blown and misshapen. Their Latin name is *contorta*. They're short and frozen in windblown shapes, some branches stripped of needles, bare and prickly.

I felt like a hobbit as I ducked through low branchy corridors toward the beach. When I broke out into open sunshine and golden sand, I chose a flat rock and spread out my picnic. I read there all afternoon. When leaning against one rock got uncomfortable, I found another with the perfect lounge-chair angle.

I had finished *Trask* and left it in Portland. All that afternoon, I read a book I'd picked out of a raggedy pile in the KOA laundromat: not a book on happiness, not a book on pilgrimage, not historical fiction with lots to think about, but a Dick Francis mystery. Clearly, my lofty pilgrimage goals had shifted, like the fall weather and the southerly drifting sun. I wasn't there anymore for the moving-on I'd feared would never happen. I was there now because...why not be there? What else would I want to do but read an entertaining book on the Oregon Coast in the sunshine, with the waves singing in my ears?

When the breeze cooled and sunlight came slanting at me from over the ocean, I pushed back through the brush to my camp, made supper, and read as I ate. The sunset was arriving earlier and closing down faster. As light faded, I put the book down. It was time to go to the beach to watch the world's daily fireworks.

A huge drift-log lay just above the tideline. I sat against it, bracing my heels in the damp sand. A woman came and sat on the other end of the log. The sky turned ever brighter gold and the setting moon more silvery with every passing second. Sea and sand reflected shards of gray and gold, and the water hushed.

I said, "WB Yeats wrote a poem. He said, 'I'll pluck 'til time and time is done/the silver apples of the moon/the golden apples of the sun.' I don't even know what that means. But it's so beautiful."

It was the first thing I said to the woman. As soon as I spoke, I thought again that I'd lost all my social graces. But it didn't seem to matter. We started talking, like old friends might, sitting on a log watching the sunset together, after one of them has broken the companionable silence.

She said, "My daddy told me, 'You're going to be tall. People think women should be small, but you are who you are, and you're beautiful.' And I always believed him."

She was carrying a camera with a huge lens. She told me she was a wildlife photographer, especially bears. "If you want to get married again, go on bear photography excursions. The men who love bears all *really* want to get married."

A camera, bears, another husband—they sounded equally unlikely.

She had lived in pain for four years, she told me. Doctors couldn't find the cause. "One even told me to go to a shrink because the pain was all in my head. But it wasn't. It was a slow-growing cancer."

I understood then how it was that we could meet each other so directly, there on a log at the Bayside campground. When life roughs us up, we learn to hold each other's pain.

The sun set. The color in the sky went on and on. She said she wouldn't forget me: Caroline from Oregon.

I went back to my burrow, snuggled in my sleeping bag and finished Dick Francis with my headlamp. I didn't bother to write down the title in my journal—just one of many Dick Francis books. But as I lay back in the dark, I felt a surge of euphoria. *That was not a book about crime but about friendship.*

I laughed at the irony—was I going to have to tell people my biggest pilgrimage insight had come from Dick Francis, not David Whyte, not Bill Bridges? That, itself, had to be a message from the sages—*Let go, for pity's sake! Lighten up!*

In my eight years of boarding school, the good and the bad years had had nothing to do with boys. Boys had come and gone, but what had mattered was a best friend. And friendship is the best part of romance, of marriage, even of parenthood. It took a long time for the endorphins to drain away and let me sleep.

I woke feeling ordinary again the next morning. I was disappointed that the glow of insight could fade that way as I slept.

In the gospel of John, Jesus took his three closest friends up on a mountain to pray. Moses and Elijah appeared and walked with him.

Peter cried out; *Let's build three tabernacles for the three prophets!*

But a voice came from heaven. *Shut up and listen.*

Not those exact words.

I sat at the picnic table to meditate. The day before had brought me friends, laughter, and encouragement. Relaxation and recreation. Why did I need to grasp it? I could feel my joy, lose it, and walk on, knowing it would all be back.

The places that felt so empty in my life would more and more fill. I would have attention again for writing. I would have dancing, and the trip to Ethiopia. I would learn to accept help. I would make new friends, like Sandy from Texas. And what I called God—that reassuring presence of power greater than my own—would continue with me.

My destination for the next night was a campground somewhere on Cape Perpetua, on the other side of the town of Yachats. My OCT map didn't show a campground, but it hadn't shown one at Beachside, either. Back in Portland I'd stressed about it. I'd looked it up. A campground shouldn't be so elusive. Now, the Cape Perpetua campground felt like a stand-in for my future. And what wisdom had I received about that? *Wait. Trust. Keep moving forward.* I set out on the five beach miles to Yachats, confident that the campground would show up for me.

As I walked, I entertained myself with memories of the year I was sixteen, when we'd stayed a week in Yachats during a US-visit from Ethiopia. Dad had spent the year studying anthropology at Fuller Theological Seminary in Pasadena. From small boarding schools overseas, I'd been dumped into an overflowing high school—Boomers coming of age. The parking lot was covered with mobile classrooms. Racial tension from the 1964 Watts riots simmered in the hallways. I spent the year with three thousand kids and not one friend.

Yachats that summer had felt remote and beautiful to me, the way Maji, Ethiopia was remote and beautiful. My sisters and I had been obsessed by tiny agates we found on the Yachats beaches. We filled our pockets with them, rounded by the surf like droplets of gold. I was eager now to see if the beach was anything like I remembered—pockets of sand nestled between black lava rocks, the sand scattered with jasper, dolomite, and agate pebbles, as though giants had turned their pockets inside out and discarded the crumbs.

That long-ago summer, I had a new, eye-popping yellow swimsuit with white piping and boy-shorts legs. My sisters and I played on the beach with a kite. My efforts to master our new skim board brought two local boys over. They tutored me on the skim board, flew the kite with my younger siblings, and rescued it when it went down in the courtyard of a small motel. "Don't worry, we know the owners," they said.

I was flattered by their attention, but nervous. Any boys I'd flirted with in boarding school, I already knew well. These boys were strange beings, real Americans. Oregon natives. They wanted to show me the sea lion cave.

My heart pounded as I climbed onto the old pickup truck's bench seat with boys who knew how to drive. I didn't know much about sex, but I had read *Tess of the D'Urbervilles*. I did know that a girl's life could be tragically ruined forever by a man.

The sea lion cave was wet and dim. It smelled rank, of fish and salt and poo. Honking sea lion cries ricocheted off the shiny black walls.

All the way home, I worried. What if the boys kidnapped me? Mom hadn't even asked their names. What if we had an accident on that narrow, cliff-edged road? How would police identify me? How would they find my parents? I didn't know my address at the cottage in Yachats. When the boys dropped me off, I thanked them breathlessly and ran inside.

A postcard from one of the boys reached me in Addis Ababa, after I got back. A postcard of the sea lion caves. The swirling emotions of that day had swept back over me as I stood in our living room in Ethiopia and studied the dark cave, the outlines of barking sea lions.

I was also baffled by the Yachats boy's effort to connect across the eleven time zones. Americans in Ethiopia came and went at the whims of administrators in the United States and of the Ethiopian government that issued work permits. I was used to separations; I was used to *out of sight, out of mind.*

That's what happened to Mark and me when we separated for college after our senior year together. But when I met up with him again in Washington DC, he made it clear he wasn't leaving this time. My childhood was familiar to Mark, not bizarre, exotic, or conversation-stopping. With him, I never had to explain how foreign I still felt—then, and even decades later. Why I sweated through games of Trivial Pursuit, unable to hide all the cultural gaps that no amount of research would ever fill in. Why I still stumbled over idioms in English; why I'd once called O'Hare Airport in Chicago an airstrip; or why some feelings could still only be expressed by an Amharic word.

And so, we'd married. Mark had been utterly loyal. He might chafe and complain, but we both knew he had it in him to open up only once, and I was the one. I could do my coming and going, the pattern I'd learned from a childhood of boarding schools and transatlantic relocations, but he'd always be there to come home to. With Mark, I would never feel a stranger, and I would never be left alone.

Over forty years later, coming to a pebbly alcove on the beach, I laid my pack aside. I picked up half a dozen agates and something that looked like the fossilized shard of a shell.

The ancient pebbles clinked solidly against each other as I dropped them into my pocket. When I set out again, I slipped my hand in to find them, worn round and slippery smooth by saltwater beating them against each other and against the sand. Over time, Mark and I had also smoothed each other over. But he, a *person*, someone who had been closer and more real to me than the physical world, turned out to be evanescent.

I passed along the ocean side of town, peeking into the edges of people's lives: tiny wind-battered cabins with crabgrass lawns, patches of rangy daisies, and bright geranium pots. Cute little blue and yellow OCT signs pointed the way at every intersection, also referring to Trail 804.

The trail runs along a low bluff above the ocean. For as long as three thousand years, Native peoples had walked on the footpath that skirts the tumble of black lava boulders along that part of the coast. Settlers widened it for buggies and later Model Ts. Everyone had used County Road 804 until Highway 101 was built slightly inland.

Later, a long fight began, one that went all the way to the Oregon Supreme Court—could private landowners fence off a public path that had run by long before they bought their parcels of beachfront land? The landowners claimed that County Road 804 had fallen out of use and lost its right of way. But the track was still being used as a favorite oceanside walking path. It was finally wrested back from un-public-spirited hands in 1990. To preserve its use by one and all, the ancient footpath was declared a public park, undoubtedly the longest, narrowest public park in the world.

Trail 804 has a right-of-way along the grounds of a hotel. It meanders above a spot where waves are forced into such a tight crevice between huge basalt boulders that high tide powers the water into an explosion of salt and foam.

Nearby, a bench bears a plaque commemorating two men in their twenties who were swept off the rocks in 2011 by a sneaker wave. Strong as the young men were, neither could find footing to clamor back up. They both died of hypothermia in a matter of minutes.

Further along, the tumbled boulders suddenly changed into softer, grayer sandstone. Turnstones swirled in the surging water. The sea and the stone that is their host have ground their corners off. They spin relentlessly, hour after hour, eroding burrows around themselves.

It was hard to face the mystery of water's power and how frail we are in it. I felt a chill, like the ancient Hebrews, who used images of the sea as metaphors for the frightening chaos of life.

Chapter 26

I walked out the other side of Yachats on a frontage path along Highway 101, past the last of scattered homes, past erupting stands of Himalayan blackberries, past elderberry shrubs, and into a wind-twisted forest of Sitka spruce. The walking wasn't hard, but I'd done my eight comfortable miles for the day by the time I came to the trailhead at the foot of Cape Perpetua.

A sign announced, *Amanda's Trail*. Who was Amanda? I began the steep climb feeling cynical. Amanda had become such a popular name when Miriam was young. I assumed some wealthy family had paid the park system to have a trail named after their daughter.

A mile and half in, I came to a grotto. The statue of a Native American woman was tucked into a space in the cliff wall of stone, ferns, and moss. I researched Amanda's story when I got home.

In the 1850s, Indian Affairs officials worked out treaties in the Western Oregon Territory with Native peoples: the Umpqua, Athapaskans, Calapooya, Molalas, Chasta, Chinookansq, Siletz, Tillamook, and Clatsop. They were moved onto a huge L-shaped reservation that ran up the coast, along the miles I'd been walking for the last month, and then inland.

Native peoples were being moved off their lands because word had gone out to the Eastern U.S. states about Oregon's fertile Willamette Valley—land flowing with milk and honey. All you had to do was get over the mountains with your oxen and your wooden wagon. Landless immigrants, adventurers, Southerners fleeing the Civil War's aftermath, they all saw new hope in land grants in Oregon Territory. We usually call these settlers by the more romantic term pioneers.

Between 300,000 and 400,000 of them poured along the Oregon California trail that veered north out of Missouri and ran through Nebraska and Wyoming, splitting at the border of what is now Idaho. The California Trail headed south, through Nevada and Utah; the Oregon Trail swung north across the Blue Mountains. For a while, between them, Southern Oregon Territory remained a blank delta on maps, known only to a few trappers and the Native peoples who had lived there for millennia.

And Amanda was not some rich suburban daughter. She was a blind Native woman in Southern Oregon Territory, the common-law wife of a settler, the mother of a young girl.

It was the California gold rush, starting in 1848, that brought settlers flooding down from Oregon. As they passed through the untouched miles of Southern Oregon cut down forests and trampled berry fields and root-crop meadows. Game animals were wiped out as gold-rushers shot their own suppers enroute. The delicate balance between the people and the land, developed over thousands of years, was destroyed. And the flood of settlers never abated.

Violent confrontations got more frequent and more violent. The territory governor wanted to solve the problem by simply removing Native peoples and ignoring the treaty that protected them.

In 1855, Oregon's bloodiest chapter opened: the Rogue River Wars. It only took one year of armed resistance before the Native peoples, starving and outnumbered, had to surrender. Two large boats carried hundreds to Portland, where they were transferred to an inland reservation. The following February, another band was marched north, a trip of thirty-three days in the cold, wet coastal weather.

A lieutenant who witnessed the removals wrote, *It almost makes me shed tears to listen to them as they totter along.*

These beaches and coastal headlands were the Oregon Trail of Tears. I hadn't heard it, or of the Rogue River Wars.

Throughout the 1850s, local militias calling themselves *Exterminators* made a specialty of rounding native people up and turning them over to the army. Over time, the Coastal Indian Reservation became home to twenty-seven groups of Oregon Native peoples, even as government proclamations reduced the land granted to them from over fifteen hundred square miles to two hundred.

Amanda was a Coos woman, dragged by militia from her husband, her daughter, and her home. It is in the written record: she made her husband promise to teach the child to read. She must have hoped reading would give her daughter some agency in life, some power to determine her own fate.

The young corporal on that march north kept a journal, and that's how we know the story. The Indian agent complained they were making only about ten miles a day because of accommodating the blind and barefooted Amanda. It was going to take ten days and cost too much to get them to Yachats, he said. He proposed leaving Amanda to starve along the way.

We know Amanda made it to Yachats. The corporal turned her over with the other survivors to the Bureau of Indian Affairs, and her story went dark until a trail developer discovered the corporal's journal in 1984. The out-and-back trail from the base of Cape Falcon was dedicated to the memory of Amanda's forced march from her home. The corporal wrote that her feet were so torn by the rocky trail that they bled as she walked.

The statue's wooden eyes are blank. People have adorned the gray woman with necklaces, beads, and feathers. Her face is raised, as though asking of God, *How can you allow this?*

A sign near the statue reads, *The Amanda Trail today commemorates the dark events of Oregon's transition from Native domain to U.S. statehood. It is through the recognition of these events that the new communities and the original peoples are coming together to restore native ways in the modern world.*

I don't question honoring Amanda. But I haven't noticed many native ways that have been restored in my modern world.

In the summer of 2020, George Floyd was killed. Demonstrations turned bitter in downtown Portland. Racial unrest swirled around the country like the water powering turnstones on the coast.

Ever since the 70s, when I first woke to it, I've used my sense of how laws and culture undergird sexism to understand how laws and culture undergird racism. Roman law gave men legal ownership of their slaves, their wives, and their children. The European law of coverture subsumed the identity of a married woman into her husband's. A Harvard Law School posting online explains it this way, *Like marriage, slavery denied women a separate legal existence.* Black men got the vote in 1864 with the 15th amendment. The 19th amendment, extending equal rights to women, was finally ratified over fifty years later.

Each English, Irish, German, Welsh and French man who came to the shores of the New World looking for a chance to start over could legally treat his wife and children's bodies as he wished. And he owned their work. By the time these men entered the swirl of Africans, Native peoples, Chinese and Mexicans in this country, centuries of European cultures had given them so much practice in domination.

And what of the women? It stands to reason that centuries of insecurity and fear made them feel vulnerable. Racism, then, benefitted them, gave an edge up to their children. It's a dark strand that binds humans together in a braid of dehumanization, each to each.

I put one foot in front of the other, back on the steep path. I may fight shame forever. As a privileged child in Ethiopia, surrounded by people living in poverty and physical hardship, I had always reproached myself. Why couldn't I be braver? Why couldn't I be more grateful? Why did I let my feelings sweep me away, when really, I was so lucky?

And mostly, why didn't I do something about the suffering I had witnessed? My shame has never done anyone good. I know that. But knowing has never helped.

Encased in fragile flesh, we all suffer. There are no protections for anyone. There is no warning. And when suffering, over large or small events, sweeps our feet out from under us, we don't know how to right ourselves. We search for hope. We reach for help. Some people do their best to respond. The lieutenant had protected Amanda from the Indian Agent. He couldn't right the wrong, but he saved her life.

Is it ever enough?

By the time I got to the end of Amanda's Trail at the top of Cape Perpetua, I was exhausted, footsore, and heart-sick.

Chapter 27

The steep Amanda's Trail opened out of the forest and dropped me right at the Perpetua Lookout. The ocean spread suddenly below the bluff. I stumbled over to a stone structure eight hundred feet above the ocean. I shed the pack and collapsed, sheltered as though in some medieval castle's parapet. In front, the world was made of blue—shifting shades of blue in the ocean and an open, flat blue sky. Below me, the dark green forest tumbled down the mountainside to Highway 101. And below that, even from so far above, the sheen from salt and water shone on the black basalt that lined the coast. The ocean silently struck again and again. Its white lace swirled in constant reinvention.

A sign informed me that the stone structure was built by the boys of the CCC, the Civilian Conservation Corps, around 1933, one of Franklin Delno Roosevelt's New Deal experiments to take government money and give men work. The CCC had set up camp at what is now the Cape Perpetua Visitor Center off Highway 101 below. They cut a trail up from the south and hauled in stone for the lookout. And what was the purpose? This fort on the top of a mountain was like a work of art. It existed for the beauty of it, a tabernacle for clear days like this, for looking seventy miles out to sea and forty miles north and south along the coast.

After my heart had bathed in beauty and my feet and lungs had recovered, I wandered into the park, where normal people accessed the top of Cape Perpetua. Manicured grass and concrete paths guided drivers from the parking lot to the look-out. It looked so domesticated compared to the wild cliff, the restless ocean, the rough stone fortress. It looked so sanitary compared to Amanda's Trail.

I searched for a faucet to refill my water bottle. I found no sign of one, and no signage for the elusive Cape Perpetua Campground I had been so sure would be there at the top of the cape. I should have been choosing a spot for my cozy rainproof tent in a matter of minutes. I wandered around, disbelieving, with my pack tugging at my tired shoulders.

Back at the lookout, several stone slab steps led down to a balcony seeming to hang out over space. A low stone wall protected us from the edge. I sat down on a stone bench to drop the pack again and think. When a young man came along and sat on the wall, leaned over slightly, and looked out over the ocean, I asked him.

He looked doubtful. "I did see a campground sign down at the bottom," he said. "Right off 101. It went by fast, but I think it said closed."

I gaped at him. I had never thought of campgrounds closing for the winter. But who would come to camp in the Oregon coast's winter drizzle?

"I think you can see it from over there."

I pulled the pack on and walked to the verge of the lawn, wrested from the forest and tamed with such well-behaved grass. A steep path led down off the cape. Sharp switchbacks showed through the brush—the path the CCC had cleared. Their camp had apparently been made into a campground at the bottom, off Highway 101. A driveway down there led into the forest.

A bar lay across the entrance.

The gritty determination that had propelled me to finish my trek rose up. I wasn't going to back down now. My destination was Florence, another twenty-three miles south. I could slip past the posts. All it takes to set up a tent is a small open spot.

Slowly doubts, then common sense, seeped in. The steep walk, when I was already tired. Would there be water? Would rangers come and make me pack up? What would I do then, at the end of my strength, at the end of the day?

Maybe, with fall moving in, the coast had closed to people on foot. I went back to the stone bench, heaved the pack off again and sat down. I gave the young man a slight smile.

He easily deduced my situation. "I'm heading to Yachats in a few minutes. I could give you a ride."

My mind processed slowly. I was Balaam, a stubborn prophet of the Israelites, whose path was barred. But I wasn't trotting off to no good like Balaam, just trying to finish this impulse I'd called a pilgrimage. I also didn't have an ass to ride, just Shanks pony, as they used to say. A tuckered-out pony at that. I also didn't need an ass to see the angel barring the path, warning me off, or the Lord to open my eyes. I could see this messenger of God perfectly well. He sat there on the wall, a round-faced, rather dumpy angel with a warm smile.

My own helpless little smile had made me open to the help that was there. His offer also felt like the sign I was waiting for. Permission. It was time to declare my pilgrimage done.

On the way down the cape road, Greg from Beaverton recommended a hotel in Yachats. "It's off-season. They'll have rooms," he said. And they did.

Waiting to check in, I browsed the rack of greeting cards by local artists and watched a good-looking older man checking out. I tried to see if his left hand had a wedding ring. I tried to come up with a way to start a conversation—a casual comment about travel or exploration in Oregon—but came up with nothing. He walked off.

When I explained my pack, the young receptionist said, "Wow, that's so inspiring. I'm glad I was the one on duty this afternoon!" On an impulse, I checked in for two nights. I needed to rest. I needed to say goodbye to the coast.

The next afternoon, I walked over to Ye Olde Green Salmon Coffee Shoppe and ordered a latte and a bowl of ice cream. On the wall behind their outside picnic table, a giant green salmon leapt out of the sea, splitting the water into foamy bits. In sunlight that was almost too bright to bear, I squinted out at the street, at the tiny beach-themed stores on the other side, and the stretch of salt water to the horizon, shimmering in a constant ripple of motion.

I walked from the café to where earth and water met, the waves striking again and again, sending spray ten feet in the air, creating a constant cacophony.

The coastal rocks at Yachats are not monolithic like the three arches, or Haystack Rock in Cannon Beach. They have a shattered lava look to them.

I sat again on the bench commemorating the two men who slipped off into the surf. I thought of David Whyte writing that we're drawn to waterfalls and rocky coasts, thrilling to the violence there between rock and water. He said that trauma hits us with this kind of velocity, creating this kind of shock. That the shocks of life are essential to the joy. The shores of a lake, water quietly lapping, offers us nothing, he said.

The young men who drowned in the violent water hadn't lived to see the joy that was supposed to follow trauma. I'd been knocked down but hadn't fallen in. Now, I did need some quiet water, where the chaotic ocean simply lapped and withdrew on the sand.

I walked back to one of the small gravelly beaches sheltered by a cluster of stones. Since my backpacking days were over, I filled my pocket with round, cool pebbles. Agates, water-worn and almost translucent, jasper, like drops of blood with the sheen of water on them. Just as I had when I was sixteen, I wanted to make jewelry out of them, to wrap pebbles in nets of silver and hang them around my neck or from my ears. I wanted to wear bits of the earth. Bits of my pilgrimage. But for the moment, I resisted the temptation to make a metaphor of them. I just wanted to feel their smooth coolness in my pocket.

Back at the hotel, I made myself a cup of chamomile tea and poured hot water into split pea soup powder. I ate the last of my crackers. That simple final supper tasted delicious. When I went back out for the final beach sunset, it also seemed more exquisite than any others. Both the soup and the sunset had been seasoned, maybe, with pride that I had walked and relief that I was headed home.

Cathy picked me up again at the Portland bus station. She hugged me hard. She had worried about me. The realization came to me faintly, since I was still deficient of worry about myself. The look on her face was right—my walking the OCT alone was the act of a weird and unbalanced soul. So be it. And she'd also been right, my little rental house this time did feel a bit more like home.

A week later, I drove to Bend to weekend with my boys and their families. Being with them again, a slight shift showed itself. I had changed as I put one foot in front of another. I had absorbed into myself the quiet forest, the implacable ocean. I had grieved and thought. Over and over, I had let go. The patchwork of moments had added up. They had rubbed out the illusion that if I grieved right, I could create a life that was new but felt familiar. Light had shown, not for the first time and not for the last, on the illusion I ran to for safety: that I could avoid pain if I did right.

Losses are irreversible. Mine had shot nerve pain through me like phantom limbs for a while. But now the losses were shifting around in my heart, looking for a place to peacefully co-exist with all I had retained.

I told this to Jesse, in the kitchen as we cleaned up supper together. Kenny overheard our serious tone, and joined us. I told them that I did feel a little disloyal to Mark as I accepted going on without him. My voice trembled. I told them about the vision I'd had of him reproaching me. And how I'd burst into tears, because I'd gotten to see his face. Not flat, like the memory of a photo, but alive and full of expression. Suddenly we were all three crying as we stood, leaning our hips against the countertop, sponges and dish towels in our hands.

Chapter 28

After I took my pilgrimage of closure, the DSM, a thick diagnostic manual of mental illnesses, added Prolonged Grief Disorder to their list. It was a controversial decision. Psychologists debated using six months as the marker between normal grieving and disordered grieving. They compromised with one year. Shocked, I looked up the list of symptoms. Had I been disordered?

My close-up view of Mark's death had left in my mortal body feeling vulnerable. On the trail, my body felt sturdy again. I was strong. My parts all worked together still. But how quickly that can change! Mark's body had been sturdy only six months before he died. I will never lose the horror of his physical disintegration.

I had probably not been disordered. I had cared for myself adequately. I had planned and organized my pilgrimage. But the diagnosis of disordered grief does include the words *longing* and *pining*. I had set out on my walk full of longing, full of hope for the wrong thing. I had known rationally that my life had changed forever. But that hadn't kept me from pining for the *feel* of my old life. I had come home from the walk more ready to let my life be new.

But still, I often slipped into a church pew with my sister and cried in church. A sense of eternal spirit made me feel small and frightened. And years later, one Sunday a soloist sang the song I'd asked Janie to sing with her guitar for Mark's and my backyard hippie wedding. I wept then, through the reading of a verse from the gospel of John; through a sermon about peace not as the world giveth; through the throw-back song about peace like a river. My river is even now full of whitewater.

The David Whyte pages I carried with me on my hike advised me not to bring in my strategic mind too soon. When waking in a dark wood, wholly lost, he said to keep things open. He said to expose myself to essential questions: who I am; who I am being asked to be? And that's what I did, backpacking on the Oregon Coast Trail. I moved forward, step by step, carrying a load. A narrow trail to surviving alone emerged.

I thought, when I set out, that the losses of my home and my work were only tangential. Now I understand they had made my grief more complex. They made the woods where I had lost my life partner feel darker.

Happy people have projects. Back in Portland, that line in the happiness book from the Seaside hostel library felt like a hint about where to begin my new beginning. I had to make a new home for myself. That could be my project.

I found a scraper-house close to where my siblings had clustered in North Portland. It was in such bad shape, the bank assessor at first wouldn't step inside because she said the ceiling might fall on her head. This was a project that would let me move on from Mark and still carry him with me, as I had while walking the tideline. I would feel for the solid footing with its gentle give that lay between my future without Mark and my memories of life with him. He'd remodeled three homes around us as we lived in them. He'd also brought other people's remodeling plans to me and we'd drawn their homes to scale on graph paper and moved penciled walls around together. I had watched Mark reshape spaces. He knew where the load-bearing walls were, and brought the changes alive, nail by nail.

Now I would gut the house and build it back to suit me. It was small, fit for one person exactly. I hired men who worked like Mark had—for themselves, with pride in their workmanship and word-of-mouth reputations. I gave my cozy new house cream yellow walls, for sunshine in Portland's rainy winters, and a garden in the neglected yard. I turned the basement into an apartment almost as big as my own, upstairs.

So I found my new home and a new source of meaning, but I

didn't find the new partner. I kept one photo of Mark and me in a simple silver frame on a shelf in my living room. A friend had snapped the picture at a Christmas party in Kenya. I stand, wearing a rosy red pinwale corduroy shirt, behind Mark, seated and wearing green. My hands rest over his shoulders, on his chest. We both look happy. We'd come through a rough, rough spell. My face showed the relief I felt that night, touching Mark, breathing with him.

In my new Portland life, my new home alone, new habits crept up on me. Mark and I had fought over bed-making, because I wanted it done. He didn't care and refused to take his turn. I finally gave up my resentment—if I cared so much about a made bed, I could do the making.

That fight went back to when I visited Mark in college and borrowed a pencil from his desk drawer. I could see that I'd better return it to its exact slot. Even so, he opened the desk drawer and said, "You borrowed a pencil." He'd had them all lined up with the tips pointing in the same direction, a detail I hadn't noticed.

Later in our life together, his work receipts and invoices took up residence on kitchen counters. It took a while for him to get tools put away after a project. I did laundry, but didn't put it away for him, so a pile of clean clothes always sat on his dresser. I accused him of presenting himself as a neatnik and pulling a bait-and-switch.

He said, "I felt so out of control in college, I had to organize what I could." And in the mobile-like balancing it takes to spend forty-one years together, I had compensated for absorbing his baseline of high-alert anxiety. I controlled what I could, which included the bed, the countertops.

Living alone, I had only myself to balance. I couldn't remember why I liked the look of a nicely made bed. I slept neatly, in my half of the queen size bed. In the morning, I threw back the sheet and comforter like the dog-ear on a page in one of the books that lay on every table in the house. I reversed the flip when I climbed back in the next night. Rumpled, my bed now looked inviting, maybe like a pile of woven sticks lined with feathers looks to a bird. We go back

169

again and again to where we once found comfort.

I began to cook for myself again and even in his absence, Mark influenced what I ate. He had gagged by the third bite of winter squash. I ate so much squash that first winter without him, a slight orange hue took the place of my summer tan.

Pancakes, popcorn, and spaghetti sauce were the only things he'd been willing to cook, once I retreated from the battle for kitchen equity. When they were young, the kids had loved Mark's pancake-animals. He pressed them down with the spatula so they wouldn't be too fluffy. He liked pancakes a little, well, what I indelicately called slimy, because we'd come of age with boarding school pancakes in Ethiopia. I was off spaghetti forever, and I was not going to be the widow-lady who ate pancakes for her supper.

I was also not going to be the lonely single woman who watched TV to be with her imaginary friends. It took me two years to buy my own small TV for my own small house, but then it sat on the bookshelf for months before I plugged it in. Finally, Kenny stepped in. He hooked the TV up to the internet. He gave me a tutorial on the remote control and registered me under his Netflix account.

When I had finished my house and moved in, I slowly experienced myself lighter, less brittle. But I thundered the garbage bins along the driveway, mentally shaking my fist at the Fates. After all the hard things I'd done alone, I still had no help with the garbage?

I thought I would write in my little house. All that quiet. All that solitude. Hadn't I longed for it when the kids were little? When I lived with them and their children? I tried my desk in every room and still never used it.

I streamed music through my tinny laptop speakers, because I'd given Mark's big homemade speakers to Goodwill. I rotated between oldies from my early adulthood and my funkier playlist with Mark Knopfler, EmmyLou Harris, and Bonnie Raitt. I listened sometimes to Mozart. His music lifted me. Maybe I hoped it would make me smarter.

Sometimes I just sat on my couch and looked out at the trees.

I could only remember high moments of joy, lows of despair and sorrow, as though in my life I had skipped from mountaintop to mountaintop with a few valley visits between. But my hours had always been filled, as they were now, with tiny moments that slipped by without notice. I had followed routines and done chores with my mind on other things. Or always in a persecuted snit, dragging the garbage bins.

Alone so much, my days felt endless, timeless. Eventually, I began to mark Saturdays by cleaning my house. I put on a dress for church on Sundays. And on Wednesday evenings, when it was time to take the garbage to the street, my spirits lifted a slight bit. Any routine felt welcome. I dragged my bins to the street and back feeling affection for the silly things.

I dug out my brown hiking boots and started walking again. I prowled my neighborhood, usually alone. Sometimes I drove to the bluff and looked down at the silent port of Portland and the empty dry-dock. Sometimes I walked at dusk, and looked gratefully at the moon.

Mark still showed up in a dream every once in a while, but the picture of us together that Christmas in Kenya didn't turn up when I moved again. It's here somewhere, but I don't need it to know that our genes will be mixed forever. Science shows that in our forty-one years together, we changed each other's DNA. And I see him in Jesse's face, in his thin strong arms. I see Mark's mother in petite Miriam, who people say looks like me. And Kenny attacks problems the way his dad did.

I kept two warm shirts of Mark's—one flannel, one corduroy. I reach for them like jackets on autumn or winter days. I used to do that on the farm in Salem. When Mark went to wear one of those shirts again, he hollered if I'd left the sleeves rolled up. I don't ever bother to roll the sleeves down any more. But to me, those shirts are still Mark's. And my kids and I will forever miss his fix-it advice when we have problems with our houses or cars.

I thought, when I started my long walk, that invoking the word

171

pilgrimage was turning everything metaphorical. In part, I was wrong about that. A challenge so physical, undertaken in such an emotional state, opened me not only to metaphor but to the hidden spirit in creation. On the Oregon Coast Trail, I saw how the physical world is both solid and filmy with spirit. Full of reassurance. Ready to minister.

Now, when I'm lonely, I lift my eyes to lift my emotions. I look at the water floating overhead, that incongruous quirk of nature. We have plenty of clouds in Portland. They never fail to relax my anxiety and land me back on earth, in the benign moment.

I set out on my pilgrimage exhausted from the churn of my grief and my anxiety over an unknown future. Along the Oregon Coast Trail, the ocean's music soothed me. When I climbed across ancient headlands, as I breathed in the trees breathed out, peaceful and strong. They taught me about leaning. And along the way, people were kind.

But it was the tideline's lessons that I really needed. I didn't understand it at the time, but what I found on the first day, on the beach at Fort Stevens State Park, gave me a way to think about my best path forward. How it would be possible to balance the memories and spirit of Mark while also moving on into my own life in his absence.

As I walked, if I ruminated on my memories, I veered too close to the ocean. The sand washed away, and I lost balance. An incoming tide pushed me up the beach, into sand that had dried. There, trying to move forward without my memories, sand slipped under my weight. Every step was sluggish.

But along the ebbing tideline, the ocean dropped its treasures: broken sand dollars, bits of agate, shards of glass now finely etched, their edges no longer sharp. Only along the tideline, did the sand give gently underfoot. Only there, did the beach hold my weight.

Acknowledgements

Thank you to Jessica Powers, at Catalyst Press who made me wiser by giving me the chance to share my experiences. She always invited me to go deeper. And to others at Catalyst Press--Karen Vermeulen for her winsome cover art, and Henry Trotter for editing and for my title.

To Janie. Instead of a friend who is closer than a brother, she has been a sister who is closer than a friend. Whenever I faltered, she believed I had it in me to go deeper.

To my true friends and fellow writers in Fat Friday, who again and again read sharply enough to see where I was trying to go and help me find ways to get there.

To Bonnie Henderson, who guided me along the way on the OCT, and let me use her as a foil as I wrote about my experience.

To all the donors, mostly Presbyterians, who made it possible for me to start a nonprofit and continue to go back to Maji. To Paul, and Chris, and Welela, my board members who saw my heart tugging me back to Maji and helped me get there. Together we support Ethiopian colleagues who are improving the lives of thousands.

And to my children, Miriam, Jesse and Kenny, who have tolerated having their imperfect family written about by their imperfect mother, and have loved her anyway. Together we gave Mark the family he hadn't been sure he'd ever have. You're wonderful wise adults, my dears, and I love you.

www.ingramcontent.com/pod-product-compliance
Lightning Source LLC
Jackson TN
JSHW021945080625
85606JS00007B/43